STEP BY STEP

a courageous journey to freedom

BY
L.D. ERVIN

TURNER PUBLISHING COMPANY

Turner Publishing Company

TABLE OF CONTENTS

The ultimate measure of a man is not where he stands in moments of comfort, but where he stands at times of challenge and controversy.
Dr. Martin Luther King, Jr.

May 1963 was a time of turbulence and change in Birmingham. There was a court injunction against demonstrations, and Police Chief "Bull" Connor was discouraging participation in Civil Rights protests by jailing those who violated city laws and ordinances. It was in this climate that Reverend Fred L. Shuttlesworth and Dr. Martin Luther King, Jr. made the difficult decision to use student protesters. One thousand children gathered for this purpose on May 2 at the Sixteenth Street Baptist Church, where meetings of the Civil Rights movement were routinely held. Over 600 were jailed before the day was over. A thousand students gathered at the church again on the next day, and Chief Connor responded with a massive force of policemen and fire trucks equipped with monitor guns that could knock bricks loose from mortar or strip bark from a tree at a distance of one hundred feet. As the children left the church, firemen pounded them with monitor guns at close range, stripping clothes and skin from their bodies. Four days later a monitor gun was directed at Reverend Shuttlesworth as he marched with a group of singing children, lifting his body from the pavement, slamming him into the church and pinning him against the wall until he collapsed. A meeting with a representative of President Kennedy on the next day led Dr. King to announce a one-day moratorium on demonstrations. But Reverend Shuttlesworth, who had been hospitalized because of injuries caused by the monitor guns, had another battle plan. As a result of Reverend Shuttlesworth's vision and tenacity, the Birmingham demonstrations set off a sequence of events that led to the passage of the Civil Rights Act of 1964. Four months after Reverend Shuttlesworth's heroic stand, the Sixteenth Street Baptist

Church was bombed, killing four girls as they changed into their choir robes and prepared for Sunday School.

Thirty-two years later, over one thousand law enforcement officers gathered in Birmingham for the 19th Annual Conference of the National Organization of Black Law Enforcement Executives (NOBLE). There is a certain irony in this since one of the first initiatives of Reverend Shuttlesworth when he returned to Birmingham in 1953 was to contact Southern cities with black officers and solicit their support for the integration of the Birmingham Police Department. There is further irony in that it was during NOBLE's Memorial March (which culminated at the Sixteenth Baptist Church) that Doug Ervin was blessed with the inspiration to tell the story of the sacrifices and contributions of Reverend Shuttlesworth. It has been said that even the fiercest army can be resisted, but not an idea whose time has come. It is time for this story to be told.

Robert L. Stewart
Executive Director
National Organization of Black Law Enforcement Executives

In Appreciation

The writing of this story could not have been possible without a cast of supporters who played significant roles in preparing me for this task. It is impossible to recognize and thank everyone who has contributed, knowingly and unknowingly, towards this effort. Any success that may be gained or realized is due to their unselfish support and patience in helping me grow as a person, student, and one of God's servants.

To the staff and faculty of Washburn University, Topeka, Kansas – thank you for opening my eyes and providing me with the vision of further opportunities that could be available through the completion of a college education.

To Paul Hahn, Chair, Department of Criminal Justice (retired), Xavier University – I am indeed grateful to you for the constant full-court pressure you applied during the summer of 1991 that resulted in my enrollment in Xavier's Criminal Justice Graduate Program. Your concern for my continued professional and academic development was crucial in my spiritual growth and my subsequent enrollment in Cincinnati Bible College & Seminary.

To Professor Jack Cottrell and other staff members at Cincinnati Bible College & Seminary – for your exemplary standards and relentless demand for excellence, and your role in nurturing and nourishing my continued faith journey – please accept my utmost gratitude.

To the men, women and children who endured the pain and suffering during the Civil Rights Movement – thank you for your sacrifice, perseverance and trust in God's deliverance.

To Lola Hendricks, for being my friend, supporter, confidant, and a major contributor to this project – your love and kindness are true examples how God, when the time is right, sends Angels to all of us.

And most of all to Reverend Fred L. Shuttlesworth and your family, for opening your hearts and reopening old scar tissue, and allowing me to share these historical events with a world that needs to hear "the rest of the story," – thank you.

May God continue to bless all of you – and keep you strong and committed to His truth.

L.D. Ervin

INTRODUCTION

Prior to July 1995, I had never visited Birmingham, Alabama. Furthermore, I vaguely remembered the violent confrontations spearheaded by Police Commissioner Eugene "Bull" Connor in opposition to Birmingham's black residents, who challenged a segregated and racist system. The passing of time and personal goals were factors in causing these significant events in American history to slip from my memory. However, thanks to the National Organization of Black Law Enforcement Executives (NOBLE), I was given another chance to understand the gravity of this great city and appreciate its impact in shaping the direction of civil and human rights for all people.

The National Organization of Black Law Enforcement executives was formed in 1976 during a symposium sponsored by the Joint Center for Political Studies, the Police Foundation, and the Law Enforcement Assistance Administration. The membership has grown from sixty, who formed the organization, to more than three thousand law enforcement officers at executive and command levels, criminal justice officials and professionals, and individuals with a commitment to public safety in urban communities. NOBLE is committed toward a goal of equity, professionalism and meaningful community involvement in the delivery of law enforcement services.

On Thursday morning, July 27, 1995, after spending a very fulfilling week in Birmingham at the NOBLE Conference, I boarded a Delta flight bound for Cincinnati, Ohio. The past week had truly awakened me to our nation's dark history as experienced by so many of the black population throughout our southern cities. Just 24 hours earlier, by 8:00 a.m., the temperature had soared to a sweltering 90°. That didn't stop some 1,300 NOBLE members (and guests), dressed in police or suit attire, from beginning their march through the streets of Birmingham in tribute to those who gave up their freedom (some their lives) in search of equal and fair treatment.

This lively group, consisting of some of the highest ranking black law enforcement officials in the country, flanked by a police escort, marched through downtown Birmingham. How ironic, a city that fought so hard and so long in denying the hiring of people of color, was now headed by a black police chief. This was truly a proud moment for all of us, and a proud moment for the city of Birmingham. As the group continued to march and greet a supportive and curious audience of onlookers, I became puzzled why all the cheerful conversation and excitement were being replaced with silence. Soon thereafter, the answer became very clear – our escorts were now leading the group into Kelly Ingram Park and down the stone path called The Freedom Walk.

Kelly Ingram Park was often a refuge and meeting area during the Civil Rights Movement for many protesters who spilled out of the Sixteenth Street Baptist Church. On the other hand, it was also here, in 1963, where so many young black children had come face to face with some of the most violent segregationists in the south. It was on these grounds that many of these young people had their skin ripped from their bodies, suffered painful and dehumanizing attacks from police dogs, and were brutally beaten before being dragged off to jail.

As the march proceeded through the park, a cloud of sadness and reverence was evident. Various sculptures along the pathway stood as vivid reminders of this dark past. One sculpture depicts a small boy crouching and a girl standing, both embracing themselves for a violent attack from fire department water hoses. The attack is symbolized by two water cannons taking aim at this pair of helpless children. It was an act of hostile aggression that caught the attention of a worldwide audience that witnessed these deadly weapons strip the skin from defenseless bodies. Another sculpture display shows a boy and girl standing and facing jail bars, further symbolizing the slavery of racial hatred.

The temperature had climbed to 95°, but this discomfort could not possibly compare with the pain and suffering of those who paved the way for us to march on this day. As the march slowly continued through the park, the procession was guided into Sixteenth Street Baptist Church, where this humble group joined united in an emotional memorial service. Later, my soul was touched during a tour of the church's basement museum, where on display were photos that showed the aftermath of the dreadful explosion that resulted in the death of four little girls.

Upon leaving the church, my experience was further enriched by the powerful story and messages that lay within the walls of Birmingham's Civil Rights Institute. Appropriately, a statue of Reverend Fred L. Shuttlesworth greets visitors to this historic site, located just across the street from the church. However, the statue of Reverend Shuttlesworth barely prepared me for what I was about to learn of this man and his triumph over the evil forces of racial hatred. I was overwhelmed to learn the role he played, the pain and suffering he endured, and most of all, how little he is recognized for what he gave to the Civil Rights Movement and to our nation.

And this morning, as I boarded the plane for Cincinnati, instead of being uplifted and invigorated by the NOBLE Conference, I felt tired and emotionally drained. The experiences of the previous few days had left me feeling exhausted and empty. I was searching for some way to resolve my own frustration. As I found my way to my assigned seat, I could only sit down and rest my face in the palm of my hands. Traveling aboard an aircraft at 30,000 feet had never been my favorite mode of travel, and this morning I felt even less enthusiastic about the prospect of traveling this super highway.

As I sat down in the aisle seat, I noticed two black females seated in the two seats to my right. I didn't care to speak or acknowledge their presence. I just wanted my own privacy and moments of meditation. I sat there for several minutes as crewmembers prepared the plane for takeoff. With my hands covering my face, the lady sitting next to me abruptly jarred my arm with her arm. As I looked at her, she politely greeted me and asked if something was wrong. I responded with a greeting and told her I was fine. A few minutes later, she once again jarred my arm. Realizing she was not going away, I gave her my undivided attention. But this time she wanted to know if I thought I was too good to talk to her. I felt insulted, but quickly responded that I did not feel that way at all.

However, she was not satisfied with my short answer and demanded some kind of explanation as to my quietness. I was astounded! I thought, "Who is this lady?" She indicated that she and her friend were on their way to Detroit, Michigan. I couldn't help but wonder, "Well, why did you have to be on this flight…sitting next to me? Did I really deserve this?"

Regardless, it was apparent that she was going to be a pain the rest of my flight! Well, I felt I had no choice but to explain how my experience in Birmingham had left me saddened and depressed. Therefore, I briefly shared with her the many activities that were included in the NOBLE Conference. I thought this would be satisfactory, but I was wrong! She pressed for more details, as if it was absolutely necessary for her to know about these experiences that had seemingly adversely affected me.

I attempted to explain how, although I should have been aware of Birmingham's history, I had come to realize that I was uninformed of the events that were responsible for many of my successes. Even more, I shared with her how I was totally unaware of Fred Shuttlesworth, a resident of Cincinnati, and what he gave to our nation. I felt ashamed that I, also a resident of Cincinnati, had pre-judged him for years without knowing the very first thing about him and his many sacrifices.

As we continued to discuss Birmingham and civil rights, she wanted to know what I was planning to do with all this new information that was causing me so much discomfort. I insisted that I had to write about this man's story so that others could realize and understand what I had learned. She laughed and responded that she had heard others say they too were going to write about Reverend Shuttlesworth, and after over 30 years, still there was no meaningful recorded document of his great work. Further, she noted that I was not a writer.

However, she suggested that if I was truly serious about such an undertaking, I should come and see her first. Somewhat curious about her invitation, I inquired as to how she could possibly assist me in writing about a subject of this magnitude. But this stranger, whom I had characterized as a "pest," this person who refused to allow me to bask in my own self-defeat, whom I had known less than an hour, identified herself as Lola Hendricks, and with a compassionate, sincere and assuring voice replied, "because I was Reverend Shuttlesworth's Corresponding Secretary…."

My Sincere Thanks and Gratitude
to
Jacquelyn J. Kuhens

CHAPTER 1
BIRMINGHAM: THE CITY AND THE TIMES

Not so long ago, in the old days, the South was the South, and the North was the North. Opportunity and progress were considered the North, while fear, hate and segregation were considered the South. In the North, Richard Daley (Mayor of Chicago) was the embodiment of politics, while in the South, Eugene "Bull" Connor (Police Commissioner of Birmingham) was worshipped by many and feared by others. In simple talk, it was "potatoes and tomatoes up there, and tators and mators down here."

And "Down Here," not so long ago, in Birmingham (and many Southern cities) men and women of color were being arrested and jailed daily because they wanted to enjoy and experience the dreams of every American. It was a daily battle with evil. A constant and tragic experience of continued enslavement. It was a refusal to accept or respect anyone who did not portray the European physical characteristics. It was a total disregard for the will of God. But during the 1950s and 1960s, the events in Birmingham, Alabama awakened the conscience of a nation and influenced the course of civil and human rights around the world.

At the end of the Civil War, Alabama's economy crumbled. Poor whites and freed slaves became trapped in what appeared to be a bondage of sharecropping or the poverty of the tenant farm. With the discovery of ore and coal in the northern part of the state, once again there was excitement and hope for all of its citizens. The poor took advantage of this opportunity and aggressively sought to make a living from this mountain of iron. Benefiting from the railroads, and the advantages of this valuable transit system capable of carrying coal and iron, Birmingham quickly grew with the promise of wealth and fortune. Its founding fathers, like other American capitalists, realizing this golden opportunity for financial gain, seized this chance for personal prosperity.

In the late 1800s, as the populist movement spread South, upper-crust planters and industrial magnates who controlled the state felt their political power was threatened. They countered the movement's appeal to poor whites and blacks by waving the bloody shirt of racism to pit one against the other. In 1901, as segregationists continued to take aim, they pushed Alabama to become one of several southern states to write new constitutions to take the vote away from black citizens. Among other things, segregation was a means of parceling out scarce resources.

There was an abundance of outside capital and increased economic self-interest of the city's original elite. Pure greed and selfish desires created an environment of extreme competition, which placed Birmingham's destiny in the hands of the wealthy. This historic city was built not only of iron and steel, but on hopes and dreams, and was a magnet for immigrants of all colors and ethnic backgrounds seeking a better life. But something sinful happened on the way to stardom. Something, which is nothing less than hatred and bitter racism, transformed this "Pittsburgh of the South" into "the Most Segregated City in America."

In Birmingham, as in many other cities and states, legalized segregation existed for at least a century after the end of slavery because those who challenged it knew they were jeopardizing their own lives and the lives of their families. Segregation became a custom, and the custom became a spoken and unspoken law, as white terrorists stood more than ready to enforce it.

It was a custom that was taught in school, glorified in politics, and rationalized in the press. Throughout the South, segregation laws, also called Jim Crow laws, were strictly enforced. The history of segregation dated back to Reconstruction, and although slavery was abolished, it was a means to keep blacks from exercising the freedoms whites enjoyed. It operated behind the falsehood that blacks had "separate but equal" facilities, including schools. Separate but equal schools were always separate, but never equal. Impoverished as many white schools were, black schools were much worse.

While riding a bus in the 1940s, the curiosity of young Lola Hendricks was stirred. She recalled realizing that the laws touched all aspects of everyday life, including where you ate, lived, worked, went to school, worshipped, and even where you were buried. She recalls asking her mother why they had to sit at the back of the bus when there were plenty of seats in the front. Her mother explained that those seats were for white people and that blacks were not only supposed to sit in the back, but past the sign that read "Colored." Thus, young Lola was ordered to always obey that rule. Lola, now 66, acknowledges, "at that age, it really didn't bother me. It was when I got older and realized what was happening."

But the problems of racism were much deeper. Blacks understood that they were not to make eye contact when talking to whites. It was common, and expected, for blacks to step off the sidewalk and into the street to permit whites to pass. It was further expected, and degrading, for blacks to address whites as "sir" or "ma'am." James Armstrong, who lived under segregation laws as a child in rural Dallas County and as an adult in Birmingham, reflected, "you knew all the time it was wrong, but you didn't think then like you do now because there wasn't anything you could do about it. You knew things you could and could not do. You knew the places you could and couldn't go and you knew where you were supposed to sit in restaurants and on the bus."

Blacks and some whites did object and challenge the laws that were mandated to deny blacks the equal treatment. And as expected, they were attacked, and some were killed by those who refused to relinquish their "superior" racist mentality. There were unsolved bombings, police terror, and in Birmingham, the inflexible segregationist forces of Birmingham's notorious Police Commissioner, "Bull" Connor. The black community generally moved quietly throughout their city, tense and cautious about expressing any opposition to the evil that lived therein. It had become a difficult daily ritual of roller-coaster emotions, never quite knowing what to expect in a city properly dubbed "the last stop before Johannesburg, South Africa."

And so, these were a few of the many adverse conditions facing black citizens of Birmingham when on March 18, 1922, in Montgomery County, Alabama, God presented to this troubled region, and to the world, Fred L. Shuttlesworth. Little did anyone realize that young Fred would become the greatest nightmare for Connor and all racial hatred. His memory begins in Oxmoor, a wayward coal-mining village some 10 miles from Birmingham. It was during this era that his mother, Alberta Webb, married William Nathan Shuttlesworth.

CHAPTER 2
PLANTING THE SEED

Fred's memory begins at about the age of three, after his mother's marriage to William. It was then that he, his sister Cleola, who now resides in Birmingham, Alabama, and their mother moved to the community of Oxmoor, a Birmingham suburb, to begin their new family. William had worked in the coal mines in Birmingham and now toiled almost daily with a large farm. Fred politely acknowledges that William had been previously married and had several grown children "as old as my mother," he says. Fred relates that he proudly accepted the Shuttlesworth name, recalling that "my mother said something that always stuck with me, 'son, the man who raised you is your father', and that is why I carry his name."

During the next 15 years of their marriage, the Shuttlesworth family was blessed with seven additional children, two boys and five girls. Eugene Shuttlesworth resides in Cincinnati, Ohio; Clifton Shuttlesworth and Eula Mae Mitchell reside in Philadelphia, Pennsylvania; Betty Williams resides in Birmingham, Alabama; and Earnestine Grimes, Iwilda Reid and Trusella Brazil reside in Milwaukee, Wisconsin.

Fred speaks about his childhood and the past as if they were recent events. "I have a good memory. I can remember almost everything that has happened in my life," he says. Like many southern black farmers, William rented a farm that provides Fred with many vivid memories. Although William was the man of the house, Fred's mother was responsible for the family's work ethic and discipline. Fred remembers that his mother was "strict and too much of a disciplinarian." He confesses that her strong disciplinarian upbringing "caused me to be too strong with my children, but at least they stayed out of trouble." Fred, comparing the strong punishment administered by his mother, says, "You know, if she did today what she did back then, in this society, I'd be in jail and she would be in jail too."

Young Fred, as an elementary school student, grew up plowing and working the fields, which included learning how to handle and care for a mule. "We planted and grew everything," he recalls.

"I grew up working because mother believed in making her children work." It was this kind of work ethic that encouraged Fred, at age 13, to find a job delivering papers for the *Birmingham News* and the *Birmingham Post*. Being a paper boy didn't pay very much he admits, but, "My mother didn't mind, and I delivered papers because that was something that I wanted to show that I could do," he said. Initially, his feet provided him with the required transportation for his daily five mile trek, until he was able to save enough money to buy a bicycle.

Oxmoor had been a mining town, but its mines had been worked out and its smelting plant dismantled. As Fred grew, employment opportunities in the town disappeared. What remained were two neighborhoods, one white and one black, separated by three or four miles. Fred recalls that only one white family lived in the black neighborhood, and this family was the owner of the general store. Racism, to Fred, was never an issue. "Back in those days, people accepted segregation. We did not know or recognize it. White people had the jobs, they ran the city, and they had everything," he said. Fred gave little thought to the living conditions of his family as they endured the cold, wooden floors of their wood frame house, which was supported by 10-foot wooden pillars. But he recalls very well the air that cut through the seams and cracks of those boards, and the 10-foot space underneath the house which gave additional strength to the sharp teeth of the wind and cold. He might have assumed that the presence of the family mule, kept fenced behind their home, was part of every household.

He disregarded the absence of any people of color inside the walls of the *Birmingham News*. Maybe he considered that one day he would be the primary headline in *The News*, and for the Birmingham media. Or maybe he felt that he was destined to leave his mark on the City of

Birmingham. But he gave little thought that his duties as paper boy did not permit him access to the office areas or knowledge of another *News* employee, S. Vincent Townsend. Townsend was a young aggressive reporter, who too would leave his mark on the City of Birmingham and the evils of racial injustice.

Townsend, born in Port Tamps, Florida, had come to the area as a boy in 1911 and, unlike Fred, was provided with opportunities to pursue and enjoy all the liberties God created for all of mankind. He worked his way through Birmingham-Southern College, selling stories about the school to *The News*. He joined *The News* full-time in 1923, became known for his aggressive and tenacious style, and was later accepted as a respected and feared city editor. He moved through the journalistic ranks as sports writer, assistant sports editor, managing editor, executive news editor, managing editor, executive editor, vice president and the assistant to the publisher of *The News*.

During the 1950s, *The News* had participated fully in what historian Robert G. Corley has called, "Birmingham's Consensus for Segregation." In Birmingham, and throughout the South, extreme efforts were made to preserve segregated businesses and institutions, in spite of the 1954 Brown v. Topeka Board of Education decision, whereby the United States Supreme Court outlawed segregation in schools. *The News* supported the efforts of local white businessmen, lawyers and political leaders to circumvent the Brown decision and maintain racially separate schools. Both local newspapers publicly campaigned for continued segregation in public parks and on buses.

Fred, speaking with candor and a lack of concern for the difference in social, racial and economic justice, recounts faithfully walking miles on his paper route morning and night, earning money to buy a bicycle. And he used his newly acquired two-wheel vehicle to pedal into Birmingham and past the food distribution office on 24th Street. It provided him with transportation to further witness the many racial and cultural barriers he would personally challenge. And perhaps no other barrier gave greater symbolism or a more constant reminder of the division between the races than the "white and colored drinking fountains and rest rooms." His travels allowed him to experience the richness of the iron ore mine, with dreams of possible employment.

Although the mine was a major employer of blacks in the Birmingham area, blacks were relegated primarily to manual labor jobs. He could travel to the vibrant black district of Fourth Avenue and enjoy the cultural excitement of the Carver Theater. At Carver, blacks could see movies made by and for a black audience as well as mainstream movies, and they didn't have to sit in the balcony.

The important Oxmoor Negro neighborhood institutions consisted of an elementary school and three churches: Saint Matthews African Methodist Episcopal (AME), Shady Grove Baptist, and Springfield Baptist Church. Fred's mother was deeply rooted in the AME church. Her father was a Steward there, and she felt that Fred and her children had a duty to continue that tradition. And just as his mother believed in her children working, she also believed in the church and in the spirit of God. Fred reflects, "in Oxmoor, there was not much to do but work the fields, play ball, ride bicycles, and let the day go by." And yes, going to church regularly was mandatory. Fred joyfully expounds, "I could not have done what I did without the church. Through the church, God led me to change the paths of Birmingham."

Fred received his primary education at Oxmoor Elementary, where three and four classes were conducted in one room. Israel Ramsey was the school principal, recalls Fred. "He was a great influence in my life. He was modest, humble, and most of all, he had the key ingredient of being a Christian." In addition to being the principal, Mr. Ramsey taught a Mathematics class. Fred recalls, as an eighth grader, he was placed in a ninth grade class taught by Mr. Ramsey. Some of the older boys were having problems with their mathematics, but, "I was always very apt and did not have to do serious study to get good grades." So, Fred anxiously attempted to answer questions the older students were unable to answer. "I was wanting to show them that I knew the answers," he said, but Mr. Ramsey refused to allow Fred to answer. He was concerned about the pride of the older boys, and "I respected him for that."

Perhaps no other teacher had a greater impact on his life than Mrs. Windham, who taught seventh, eighth and ninth grades. "She was light-skinned, and when she gave me whippings, she became red." But Fred credits her for "making me get my lessons." As he cheerfully smiles, he readily admits that he was a mischievous student. His anti-social and disruptive behavior seemed to have been a way to obtain her attention and approval. It was the kind of behavior which often elicited whippings from Mrs. Windham.

For instance, the change and dismissal of classes were regulated by a clock, which included the sounding of a bell at certain hours of the day. On one occasion, Fred wanted school dismissed early, so while standing in a corner as punishment, he turned the hands on the clock forward, which resulted in the bell ringing ahead of schedule. Thus, when the bell sounded for dismissal of school at 3:00, Mrs. Windham assumed it was indeed 3:00. But when she realized that it was only 1:30, she immediately knew that Fred was the culprit.

"She took me in the room and began whipping me with this little strap," he said as he held up his index finger, indicating the size and shape of the strap. She continued whipping Fred in an attempt to get him to show remorse by crying, but Fred had trouble responding to her expectations. "I refused to cry because I didn't want the girls to see me crying," he said. At various times, she would stop whipping him, expecting the punishment was severe enough to elicit tears, and send him out the door. But each time, when Fred did not cry, she would bring him back in the room and whip him again. She whipped him so long, and repeatedly in the same place, that indentation marks were left in his skin. Finally, after about the fifth whipping, "I realized that if I don't cry, this woman was going to kill herself and me too." So to appease Mrs. Windham, and save himself from possible injury, Fred placed some spit underneath his eyes, which satisfied her desire for Fred to show tears.

In 1937, after graduating from junior high school, Fred enrolled in Wenonah High School and walked several miles daily to and from class. The following year he transferred to the Rosedale High School, and in 1940, graduated as Valedictorian of his class. Fred talks of the high admiration he had for all his teachers. And rightfully so, for they seemed to have played significant roles in sparking his ambition and motivation to provide social change. Their watchful eyes and discipline ignited a flame which continues to burn in his memory. "I believed in them and they believed in me," he said. He credits Mr. Ramsey, Mrs. Windham and others as the people from whom he learned to analyze things. "They helped me to deal with some of those Southern politicians. I learned from my teachers to pay attention to what they do; not what they say," he adds. The country community of Oxmoor gave credence to the African proverb, "It takes a village." Teachers, preachers and parents participated in the growing process of all children. He recognizes that "there were no great people to do little things. But there were a lot of little people who did great things."

Fred had no specific plans or dreams during his childhood. However, the dramatic personalities of preachers left a lasting impression on him. His emotions were stirred by their ability to preach and pray. They seemed to have a special dialogue with God – the kind of dialogue and communication which could leave a positive impact on the world. Although he often considered becoming a doctor, his emotional responses to their ministry led him to believe that he was called to preach. However, that was not the first thing on his mind. "I felt I wanted a brick house, and I wanted to get married," he said.

In 1940, two days after graduating from Rosedale High School, the man he had recognized and accepted as his father died. The years of working in the mines resulted in a severe lung illness. William had provided for his family through the long and hard work of farming and welfare, but he was often sick. Fred admits, "He was a sick man, he coughed a lot, and he cursed as much as he coughed."

CHAPTER 3
LEAVING HOME

Following his graduation from high school, Fred continued to live at home, but he focused his future on nearby Birmingham. He began working at the Old Southern Club, Fifth Avenue at 20th Street in Birmingham. It was a place where poor people were given physical and economic evaluations to determine their employment aptitudes. He performed various duties in the offices of the doctors. In one office, 19-year-old Ruby Keeler was employed as a nurse's assistant. Ruby was finishing her last year in nursing at Tuskegee Institute and was working there for the summer. And what began as mutual admiration quickly resulted in their constant companionship. However, at the end of the summer, and to Fred's surprise, Ruby decided that she did not want to return to classes. Fred was surprised even more to learn that she wanted to get married.

"I did not want to get married," he reflects. But apparently, after meeting Fred, Ruby did not want to return to Tuskegee and decided she would rather spend the rest of her life with Fred. Fred felt obliged to assist his new love. To ease the pain and disappointment of their parents, they told them that Ruby was pregnant. However, Ruby was not pregnant, and according to Fred, "I had never touched her and didn't until the night we actually became engaged. Now, I had touched some others, but I had never touched her."

With a wife, Fred decided he needed a better job. He found a job at the Alpha Portland Cement Plant which paid $4.52 per day. Because of the complexity of his assignment, he was making more money than workers who had been on the job for 16 years. With his job, and Ruby's job in a doctor's office, they were able to buy a house from William Croom. Fred also took advantage of a government training program at the Fairfield Hayes Aircraft plant, where he began classes in automobile engine repair. It was through this training that he learned about a possible job in engine repair at a military facility in Mobile, Alabama. In 1943, interested in making more money and seeking better opportunities, he and two friends traveled to Mobile, where they applied for a job in the defense industry at Brookley Air Force Base. On the same day they applied, they were accepted for employment.

Ruby soon joined Fred as he began his new venture as a truck driver and later a machine operator at the base where he would labor until 1947. Fred had no regrets about having to leave the "boom town" of Birmingham. His family and friends were there, but now he had a new family, and in Ruby, he had found a new friend. She had provided him with the satisfying experiences of parenthood, love and companionship. He was proud of being able to make good and positive decisions, and staying away from the "wild and rowdy crowds." But he was also proud of his rich and deep spiritual roots. Although he had "felt a call" to minister, he felt that he could enter the ministry at his own pace, and then make his call known.

He directed his sights first on making a home for his family. The military facility in Mobile was involved in remodeling government buildings. Shuttlesworth noted that whenever a building was demolished, the lumber and supplies were destroyed or thrown out. Fred, realizing the value of another man's junk, seized upon the opportunity to build the house he had always wanted. Having access to a truck, he began hauling salvage lumber to a chosen building site, and with the assistance of members from Corinthian Baptist Church, constructed a house for his family.

The Shuttlesworth family had been Methodists at Oxmoor, so he began attending a Methodist Church in Mobile. He can't explain why, but recalls that in the Methodist Church, there was a certain "chill and cold" that did not allow him to "get the spirit." At the encouraging of a co-worker, he began visiting Mobile's Corinthian Baptist Church. He was pleased and invigorated with the friendliness of the congregation. Ruby had not attended Corinthian, thus he proclaimed his excitement and asked her to attend to get her impression. He and Ruby felt accepted at Corinthian and developed a feeling of "belonging."

In 1945, Fred professed his faith, joined the congregation and was baptized. These events were followed by Fred declaring his call to preach. Reverend Palmer, Pastor at Corinthian, accepted Fred's profession, evaluated his faith, and licensed him to preach. In July 1946, Fred was called to Pastor his first church in Selma, Alabama and was officially ordained. The process consisted of a board that interrogated Fred about his fitness to pastor. It was a matter of Fred convincing the board of his unquestioning Christian faith. This included Shuttlesworth's complete subscription to Baptist doctrine and his determination to uphold a high standard of morals and manners. Being satisfied with his responses, Fred was prayed over, consecrated to God's service and awarded an Ordination and Certificate, declaring him acceptable as a witness for God through preaching. In essence, he had been granted a license of major significance. However, he realized that he was still lacking the skills in many areas to adequately carry out his call to the ministry.

Although he was lacking in formal education and theological training, Fred, ignited with enthusiasm, set out in a devoted study of the Bible. As a truck driver, he felt he had been blessed with a job that allowed him a lot of free time. And he used every bit of that time to his benefit. As he continued to read and study his Bible, he realized that he was seeking a greater light and better understanding of God's Word. What he was lacking in educational experience, he made up for with enthusiasm.

Apparently, he was well-liked. His eyes gleam with excitement as he recalls his ordination. He recalls the experience this way: "I felt like a jet being lifted off the ground. It was like wings opening up for me. I began preaching everywhere." Reverend Palmer also relied on Fred to preach in his absence from Corinthian Baptist. Fred remembers a specific absence and how the deacons attempted to take advantage of Fred in uniting the congregation against Reverend Palmer. They were trying to organize a meeting to be held following church services to further their cause. Their basic goal was to "vote out" Reverend Palmer. As for the reason, he explains, "People don't need a reason. There is always something they don't like about you. If they feel like they can do something better, they will try to exert their influence." As Fred reflects on many of his life experiences, he is convinced that, "God dealt with me in such a way that I knew it had to be Him."

Confronted with the deacon's attempt to oust Reverend Palmer, Fred was unable to relax or sleep. All night the Holy Scriptures rested heavily on his mind. Early the next morning, he went to visit several of the deacons as they gathered at another's home getting ready for work.

"I told them that Reverend Palmer was the pastor, and if they had differences, they needed to work them out with him. They wanted to hold a meeting following my sermon to complete their task of getting rid of Reverend Palmer. They told me that I did not have to participate, but they just wanted to announce the meeting to the congregation. I told them that I was only the guest preacher and I would dismiss church following service, and that I would not condone such actions by them. Although they did not agree with me, they told me that they respected me as a man. Following the church service, I dismissed the congregation, and there was no meeting."

Fred's energy and popularity kept him busy during these times. He maintained a full-time job at Brookley Field, was preaching on a regular basis, and completed self-study to improve himself. Although he had no firm direction, his life seemed to have been chartered by a higher authority. As a licensed "local" preacher, his ministry was secondary, and he was honored by the response and spiritual excitement of his audiences. The more he preached, the more people wanted him to preach.

However, there were significant pieces missing from his life. He had gone to Mobile with hope and optimism of accomplishing great things, but he found mounting difficulties. He thought he had a good job making $1.25 an hour. He was well-liked by his superiors and co-workers, but he did not see a future in his employment, and even there, he was faced with recurring problems that tested his patience and fortitude. One of his co-workers, a white Mississippian, enjoyed boasting about the control whites had over Negroes where he came from. Once he told a story how blacks could not walk on the sidewalks of his town. They had to walk in the middle of the street, and they had to take off their hats when walking through white neighborhoods. This and other stories implied that blacks knew their places, and as long as they responded as expected, whites and blacks would have no problems. Of course, black employees, feeling that any negative responses on their part would result in retaliation, remained silent.

But Fred was not known to remain silent on any issue in which there was evidence of injustice. Sensing he had a duty to respond, Fred told him they had no problems because, "you didn't have Negroes in your town with guts." Fred was a little man who weighed less that 140 pounds, but he stood tall for the common good. Before his opponent could respond, Fred continued, "I haven't been in your town, but if I ever get there, you will see a Negro with his hat on walking your sidewalks. That will be one time a Negro won't be walking in the street bareheaded."

There was another encounter when a black co-worker, with six children, was told that he would have to take a reduction in pay. The inequity of pay was evident. Fred immediately became an organizer and challenged the proposed action and military authority. In essence, Fred was instigating a strike, which was not only unprecedented, but such behavior was a basis for administrative discipline. Fred, being unfamiliar with the military and government restrictions, states, "I had no idea that we could not strike." What he did know was that there was a serious problem which needed resolving, and he was the only person willing to take on the responsibility. His actions resulted in him being reassigned to an office area away from the other employees, as well as strong counseling. However, his co-worker did not suffer a pay cut. Instead, most employees received an increase in pay.

Just when he felt his spirits low and his patience growing thin, he met an aged white couple, Dr. Maynard and his wife. The couple was impressed with Fred's desire to serve Christ, and they encouraged Fred to become better prepared for the ministry. They even promised to provide him with financial support if he would sacrifice and go to college. With their support, and his continued hunger for knowledge, Fred enrolled in Cedar Grove Seminary at Pritchard, Alabama. Not long after his enrollment, teachers and students became attentive to his oratory skills. They encouraged him to participate in an oratorical contest at Selma University, a small Negro Baptist college. Fred accepted the challenge, participated in the contest, was an overwhelming favorite, and became known throughout the area. He was spiritually and personally touched by the attention and compliments he received from the audiences. During a tour of Selma University, he was introduced to Dr. William H. Dinkins, President of the University. His conversations with Dr. Dinkins, and the overall approval rating he received, encouraged him to become a student at Selma.

Upon returning to Mobile, the experience in Selma rested heavily on his mind. He had championed the causes of ministers, co-workers and laymen alike, and yet, he was not satisfied. He had taken on no one certain crusade, and he had no crusades planned. However, his future was in the ministry, and he was determined to move in that direction. He had gone to Mobile to make money, and some three years later, "I had saved about $97, and I told my wife that I could pick up more than $97 worth of sticks in a year." As 1946 drifted by, he continued to weigh his options. During his meeting with Dr. Dinkins, he felt that he could get assistance from Selma University if he chose to enter the university. Ruby listened patiently as he shared his feelings.

"I feel like my life is to touch people," he told her. "I don't know how, but I have to go to school." His life was to touch people, and he seemed to sense that God had an even greater purpose for him. And so, being guided by his God, Fred was faced with yet another challenge that could mean resigning from his government job to "go to school."

Chapter 4

Branching Out: Preparing For Birmingham

Fred never spent too much time considering a possible course of action, and as he pondered his future, he was not about to start now. He wrote to President Dinkins and expressed his desire to continue his education at Selma. But Fred was not just another potential student – he had a wife and three children. In that day, black colleges were not equipped socially or financially to accommodate married couples. However, it appeared that God was directing the future of Fred Shuttlesworth, and Fred's faith took care of the rest. Fred submitted his letter to Dr. Dinkins when Selma University was in the process of building housing units to lodge married couples. Within a few weeks of writing to President Dinkins, he was accepted as a student.

However, Fred, Ruby and their children faced another dilemma. Fred was employed, making pretty good money, and there were no assurances that he would be successful in gaining employment in Selma. Again, Fred's faith provided him with all the assurances that he needed. And so, in 1947, he resigned from his government job, moved to Selma, and he and Ruby became the first married couple to reside in student housing. His move was not just an abrupt uprooting. As he made plans to move, he had taken his savings to buy and slaughter a cow. Fred had carefully planned to care for his wife and family. The cow he purchased was slaughtered and converted to 455 pounds of beef, which was transported to Selma in a rented truck.

Upon their arrival in Selma, he immediately arranged for the use of a freezer in the local area, to store all of the processed meat. Well, Fred had plenty of meat, but their taste buds would soon fade. "We ate beef for a long time, but after awhile we got tired of it and gave it away."

He was also faced with the problem of heating; his housing unit did not have a heating system. Fred had small children and a wife, and he knew he needed adequate heating. Using the skills he had developed in trade school, he installed his own 90-gallon propane heating system he had brought from Mobile. Fred's outgoing and jubilant personality, and his ability to adapt to a variety of adversities, quickly gained the attention of Dr. Dinkins, who was aware of the difficult task Fred and his family were undertaking.

Although Fred was securing odd jobs to provide for his family, he still faced financial hardships in trying to attend school and take care of his wife and three small children. Dr. Dinkins came to his rescue by purchasing and providing the family with a cow. Unlike the previous cow, this cow was not for slaughter, but was for the purpose of supplying milk for the children. Dinkins allowed Fred to pay for the cow by providing the school with two quarts of milk a day. Any milk in excess of the two quarts was sold to the school at 14 and 1/4 cents per quart. The cow quickly became another member of the student family. At her death, the local newspaper paid tribute to the cow by printing a story of the contributions she had made to students at Selma University.

As time passed and the needs of his family increased, Fred became unable to provide them with the essentials of life. Thus, to assist with the apparent hardships of the family, Ruby was required to seek employment with Good Samaritan Hospital, a Catholic institution. This was an apparent conflict of interest with the policy of Dr. Dinkins. Up to this point, Fred and Dr. Dinkins had developed and maintained a perfect relationship. Ruby, a nurse at the hospital, would routinely walk to work in the early morning hours wearing her hospital attire, a white dress and hat. Dinkins did not realize she was working at the hospital until their paths crossed one morning when she was going to work, and he was entering the university. In his inquiry about her place of employment, he was shocked and disturbed to learn that she was employed at the Catholic Hospital.

For some reason, "Dinkins, who served as President from 1932-50, did not think Baptists should associate with Catholics." He quickly summoned Fred to express his dissatisfaction and opposition with the fact that Baptists were working with Catholics. This authoritarian view was not accepted by Fred, who responded, "Nobody tells my wife what to do but me!" Fred recalls that Dr. Dinkins was in additional shock from his comment. "He almost swallowed his tongue, but that was my decision to make. My wife working as a nurse may have been a conflict, but not where I was concerned. It was a conflict where Dr. Dinkins was concerned." However, the matter was never brought up again, so apparently, Dr. Dinkins accepted Fred's decision.

Fred spent two years at Selma. During those years, he showed continued excitement and enthusiasm with the challenges of college and seminary studies. He took on tough courses in Greek, Latin and French, and remained confident, saying, "Those were some glorious years, and my mind could grasp anything."

In 1948, while a student at Selma, he was invited to preach at Everdale Baptist Church, which resulted in the acceptance of an offer to pastor the church two Sundays a month. A short time later, he accepted an invitation to pastor Mount Zion Baptist Church for the other two Sundays. Both churches were located in rural communities a short distance from Selma. Their congregations and financial resources were small, which meant his salary was small. But Fred was eager to preach, even though "the pay varied from Sunday to Sunday, and was never that much."

From 1948 to 1950, Fred was busy with preaching. His energetic and high-spirited messages placed him in constant demand. He was honored in having the opportunity to preach four or five times on some Sundays. But Fred was still not satisfied. It appeared, at least for the time, that the Lord had other directions for him. In 1949, there was an advertised shortage of public school teachers in Alabama. The need for teachers was so great that many applicants were being hired on teaching permits. Fred was disappointed that many "did not even meet the 'C' requirements, which was the lowest grade for a teaching certificate." Fred had a desire to teach and considered himself more qualified that many of the teachers being hired, but he did not have a teaching certificate. Further, Selma University did not offer classes that would qualify him for a certificate.

His deep respect for his primary school teachers and his positive experiences as a student had motivated him to become a teacher. Having this continued desire, Fred was determined to obtain his certificate and therefore, took his transcript to Alabama State College, where he met with J.T. Brooks, Assistant to the President. Mr. Brooks was impressed with Fred's consistent high grades and accepted him immediately. Within a short period, Fred was in Montgomery, and with a family which had expanded to four children, Patricia, Ruby Fredricka, Fred Jr., and Carolyn. He was so excited about his new adventure, he left without sharing his decision with Selma administrators. But he also felt they only would have attempted to dissuade him from leaving.

When Fred initially arrived from Selma, he became acquainted with the First Baptist Church, which Fred characterized as a prestigious church. In 1950, shortly after settling in Montgomery, he was contacted by Ben Harrison, a deacon from First Baptist Church. Harrision, Fred says, "had big, round veins that stood out from his head like ropes." He told Fred how the church had recently experienced some misconduct by its pastor, which resulted in the pastor being dismissed. The church was presently without a pastor, and was considering Fred as their interim preacher if he was willing to accept a salary of $10 per Sunday. At that time, "10 was like $150 is today." Fred preached from October 1949 until May 1950 before being accepted as the pastor.

Fred had finally achieved a goal in his quest to follow God's directions. The church was the oldest black religious institution in the county, and provided Fred with a modest parsonage for his family. However, Fred quickly had a rude awakening. He recognized that not only was the church old, "but the leadership of the church was old with old ideas." The church was run and controlled by the Deacon Board, and "the deacons were old enough to be my grandfather." Although the Deacon Board existed, the decisions were primarily made by two members, Harrison and J.D. Pritchard, "who could sing like an angel and curse like a sailor." Harrison and J.D. apparently made it clear that the board should establish control over all aspects of the church. Of course, none of this went over too well with Fred, who believed that God was using him as a positive influence and to bring about meaningful change in the lives of others. When accepting the position, Fred failed to realize that not only was the building worn and decaying, "but the leaders of the church were worn and decaying." The deacons did not allow members to vote or have access to the business of the church. They had no vision nor a desire to grow with the spirit and vigor of Fred Shuttlesworth. Simply speaking, an explosion was inevitable.

In fact, a spark of conflict was ignited almost from the beginning. However, Fred delayed the actual explosion and attempted to work through the difficult issues. It became obvious that issues would continue to grow. Members of First Baptist considered themselves "elite" and set themselves apart from others who were not as fortunate. On one occasion, J.D. approached Fred regarding his friendliness and relationships with blacks who did not meet the standards of the "front line" First Baptist members and other preachers. He told Fred, "You are First Baptist's Pastor now and you don't have to fool around with little niggers anymore." Fred replied, "God must have loved little niggers because he made more of them than he made of anybody else."

Fred was viewed as an incoming young idealist with a vision and optimism, which were too remote and difficult to digest for the old ways and conservative thinking of the deacons. The deacons made sure they reviewed all expenses, as well as the approval and signing of all checks. A peaceful resolution was not only remote, but impossible. Fred spent countless nights worrying about his ongoing conflicts and woke almost daily without getting adequate sleep. He often felt alone and without the support of his God. Now he readily submits, "God was getting me ready for Birmingham." He relates how he realized that God was really there with him.

"I was riding a train to Oklahoma for the 1952 National Baptist Convention. As it had been, I could not sleep. I said to the Lord, 'Why did you send me to First Baptist?' I said, 'I don't mind working and suffering, but I just want you to fix it so I won't worry anymore.' After that, I had a great weight lifted from me. I had no trouble sleeping that night and didn't worry about anything. That was the first time I had a real awareness of God."

When he arrived back from the convention, Fred was re-energized. He brought back his own agenda and program for the proper operation of the church. He immediately took over the signing of checks so they would not be written without his permission. He also presided over Deacon Board meetings. The deacons fought his abrupt change in policy and called for a full membership meeting to argue their case. After the church membership met to hear the argument, his procedures received overwhelming approval.

By this time, Fred's salary had reached a pleasing $180 bi-weekly. And as his salary increased, so did the conflicts. He is proud and honored to have had the support of Nora Bennett during those troubled times. He often confided in her and repeated his plea for "no trouble." Little did he realize that just being at First Baptist was trouble. Ms. Bennett cautioned him that the deacons had run off every pastor prior to his arrival, and he offered her continued support. However, as if Fred did not have major problems, an additional conflict developed due to Fred's employment as a teacher at Street Manual Training School. His opposition, objecting to his additional financial benefits, claimed that his teaching duties detracted from his ministry responsibilities. Once again, the church membership met to discuss the issue and voted in favor of Fred. Although he won another battle, it added to the existing volatile conditions.

As Fred continued his efforts of "meaningful change," his adversaries were relentless. J.D. and Harrision attacked him on every front. In another matter, the church was making plans for the construction of indoor restroom facilities. Harrison owned a plumbing company and appointed himself as the contractor for any church related repairs. Fred opposed this process on the basis of a conflict of interest, and he encouraged the deacons to solicit bids from various outside companies. Harrison and others vehemently opposed such a proposal, but a committee was established to solicit and receive all contractor bids. Proving that he was as clever as Fred, Harrison was able to get himself appointed to the committee, which allowed him access to the bids being submitted. As expected, Harrison's bid was the lowest for the construction of the church restroom.

Finally, even the reserve of Fred Shuttlesworth could no longer endure the strain of a continuous internal battle with the church members and deacons. Ms. Bennett and others had stood with him, but there was no end in sight to the many troubles that plagued this historic institution. It was an unfortunate case whereby ill-advised and misguided followers of Christ had failed to fully understand their true mission in the church. Weary and worn from the many obstacles, Fred called a church meeting one Sunday morning following service.

It was a sad day, not only in his life, but that of First Baptist. As he now recalls, "I told them I was not concerned about preaching as much as I was concerned about being a man." As he concluded and rendered his farewell, he said, "I will not stay here as pastor and allow the deacons to do what they want, while I have nothing to do." First Baptist may have lost a fighter, but Fred continued his journey as he sought to change those he touched. And as God only knew, he was not just destined to touch people in Alabama, but people throughout the world.

The door that closed on Fred at First Baptist only allowed doors to open elsewhere. His reputation generated many requests for him to preach throughout the southeast. In February 1953, he was called upon to preach a trial sermon in Florida. However, Reverend Motley, a close friend he had met in Mobile, asked him to fill in for him at Bethel Baptist Church in Birmingham. Bethel had selected Reverend Motley as pastor. However, he had not accepted the call. Reverend Motley was already pastoring a church in Mobile and found himself committed to the needs of his congregation. Fred was not impressed because he, too, had a commitment in Florida. But Reverend Motley refused to accept "no" for an answer, and quickly countered by offering Fred $40 to preach at Bethel. Now, that seemed to impress Fred, who readily canceled his Florida plans and went to Bethel.

The following week, Reverend Motley called upon Fred again, and again Fred declined. This time it was not the money. Fred had impressed the members at Bethel, and many expressed a desire for him to consider the pastorate. On the other hand, Fred respected the ministry and felt it was not appropriate for him to return to a church that was considering another minister as its pastor. Motley attempted to encourage Fred to go by saying, "It could be the Lord." But Fred was not convinced, and he insisted that he did not play with the Lord. Following additional discussion, Fred agreed to honor Motley's request. The results of his return visit were no surprise to Fred, as the members continued with more intense efforts to persuade him to accept the pastorate at Bethel.

The situation was not only in conflict with Fred's respect for the ministry, but in conflict with his code of ethics. He did not want to "burn any bridges," but he found it difficult to refuse an opportunity to pastor a church. As far as he was concerned, Reverend Motley was the pastor, and he should decide whether or not he was still interested. With this thought in mind, he told the congregation he would be willing to accept the position if, for some reason, Reverend Motley changed his mind. Armed with this information, the church leaders contacted Revered Motley and arranged a church meeting to discuss the offer. Fred sat unconcerned that evening over the outcome of a decision that would play a deciding role in the history of Alabama and the nation. "It was not just raining that night," he says, "it was really storming." It is not known what issues were discussed, but for whatever reasons, Reverend Motley did not appear. Of course, church leaders made immediate contact with Shuttlesworth, who accepted the offer and agreed to assume his duties beginning March 1, 1953.

It appeared that Fred was finally returning to his home, but there was another little matter that was unresolved. Fred, as a teacher and leader at Selma, was under a contract that did not expire until May 1953. As a matter of fact, school officials made it clear that they had no intentions of releasing him, and they were interested in retaining his services beyond May. Realizing how much the ministry meant to Fred, they proposed a compromise that allowed Fred to preach on Sundays, with a promise that he would be appointed to the first position as principal to open in the school system. Fred did not foresee such an arrangement as being productive and satisfying. Thus, again Fred was faced with making a decision that may be regarded as difficult for some. But to Fred, it was no contest. He now fully realized, "My first calling was the ministry." And as he had become accustomed, he gave little consideration to his possible options. He immediately submitted his teaching resignation and pursued "his calling."

CHAPTER 5
COMING HOME: A TIME FOR CHANGE

In March 1953, Reverend Fred Shuttlesworth and his family returned to Birmingham. It was not his desire to change the conditions of this troubled city. However, as a child growing up in rural Oxmoor, he had thought many times, "Something has to be done, but who is going to do it?" He helplessly witnessed the deputy sheriff parade through his community and "beat up on people." While employed at Brookley Air Force Base, he was offended and frustrated by the racial and social injustices. And even while teaching in Dallas County, the same ugliness was always a daily experience. He recalled his tenure as a teacher in Selma, where he helplessly watched Negro children walking miles to school through mud and fields.

He returned to Birmingham only to be faced with similar childhood memories that made it more difficult to accept. Memories of school buses that were "hand downs" from the white school students. Often these buses were in such poor mechanical condition, they barely were able to provide reliable transportation. And when they operated, students were late in getting to school. Then, there were the heavy torrential rains, which caused heavy flooding and rising waters, that added to the transportation problems of getting to school. As much as he and others wanted to be in the classroom, the high waters and lack of transportation often kept them home for weeks.

It had been some 10 years since he departed this city for a better life, and now he returned, expecting to find a raised standard of living. But after all these years, for the black populace, little, if anything, had improved. Some 20 years later, the same conditions continued to exist. Fred was determined that there was much that had to change. As he recognized himself as a possible catalyst for change, there was little thought that he would be the most significant crusader for social change and justice in the history of that city.

Still, he was excited about being back in the place that helped shape his life. The city and the nation were facing the kind of challenges that only a few people were capable of opposing, willing to risk their freedom, and their life to change. But young Fred had developed a social consciousness that had deeply prepared him for a call to action. He was well aware of struggles in life, insecurity, weaknesses, abrasiveness, crime and lack of pride. He had witnessed and experienced many of the fears and racism that existed, which presented ongoing dangers to the well-being of not only people of color, but all of society.

As he returned to Birmingham and accepted his new role as pastor of Bethel Baptist Church, Shuttlesworth was uncertain how he would pursue his mission. "It was good to be in Birmingham," he says. But it didn't take him long to react to the many illnesses of the city. Not only was there flagrant evidence of racism and social injustice, there was also a "lack of pride by blacks in the city," he says. Herman Poe, a Deacon at Bethel Baptist Church, had been in the church since his childhood. Herman and others in North Birmingham were confronted daily with black on black crimes. Not only did the police department ignore the problem, but they often contributed to it by allowing a white-only police department to beat and abuse black residents. When Fred returned to Birmingham, "the first thing he did was to focus on the crime and the police department," Herman says.

In fact, Fred was deeply disturbed. He took his concerns to the local Civic League organization and the black ministers. He began calling meetings at clubs and any facility where he could get the community to come out and listen. Fred was further disturbed that blacks were not registered to vote, appeared not to have very much confidence in the system, nor the desire to participate in the political process. He was angered that blacks were not permitted employment in retail stores, or in city, state or government offices. His initial concern was that "black people needed civic pride." Fred had established himself as a viable voice and leader, and felt he was in a position to awaken that consciousness.

His initial active bid for social change was directed at getting black people registered to vote. He began to utilize the Civic League as a primary vehicle in organizing forces for the work that had to be done. Fred had lived in other cities and enjoyed various tasks of being a champion for injustice wherever they appeared. He did not realize that Birmingham was not ready for his type of change. Nor did he realize that Eugene "Bull" Connor, Birmingham Police Commissioner, would not take kindly to blacks who opposed Birmingham's long tradition of segregation. But then, Fred didn't really care.

He saw no harm in coordinating and holding meetings of concerned citizens who were interested in bringing about positive change for their community. However, any group meeting by blacks was viewed as a threat, was not well received, and sometimes was met with violence by white citizens fearful of the unknown. Therefore, due to this fear, apathy, and complacency, people were too discouraged to comply with Fred's visions of social change. Herman recalls an early meeting at Sardis Baptist Church, whereby "even some ministers attempted to discourage participation." The city and surrounding area were blessed with more than 400 African-American churches, and Fred was appalled that area ministers (black and white) chose to remain silent, rather than expose the truth in God's Word.

But Fred pushed ahead with a more active campaign of preaching and speaking on civic pride. The best way to establish that pride was to get every able-bodied person to vote. Segregationists had strongly discouraged blacks from voting, and now it was hard to instill this "right" as a form of pride. Many did not have transportation, and many were physically unable to walk to the office of voter registration. "Often, I personally transported people to the voter registration office," he says. He added, "They were not only lacking in transportation and civic pride, but many had not been provided the opportunity to attend public schools and did not have adequate education."

Seizing this, the city responded to Fred's relentless and aggressive actions by developing an extensive written examination relating to state government that blacks had to take in order to register. Herman remembers the exams well, and says, "There were questions about the State Legislature, Congress, House of Representatives. Some questions that even they did not know the answers to." Many recall one question, "How many seeds are in a watermelon?" Not to be deterred, Fred obtained a copy of the exam and organized groups to help prepare the people for the exam. He would often transport large groups to take the exam, and if one did not know the answer to a question, the group had developed different clues and signals that could be provided to each other during the exam. Fred laughs, "Before long, we had some very lively exams and registrations." His continued fight with the Board of Election ended with Fred filing a law suit to eliminate the exams and to allow unchallenged voter registration to black citizens.

As Fred's popularity grew with his black supporters, it diminished with his opponents. A large part of the problem was, in part, due to an all-white police department and the abuse inflicted upon the black community by white officers. Now it was time to meet the "Bull" (Connor) head-on as Fred fixed his sights on getting black policemen appointed to the city's police force. He recalls an early meeting with Mayor James Morgan, who indicated he was in support of hiring black officers. Morgan also expressed his displeasure with the current social problems in the city, including school segregation. Apparently, Morgan talked a good talk. Nevertheless, it didn't take Fred long to realize that Morgan was "just talk," and he never cared, nor intended to do anything to meet the needs of black citizens. Simply, this was Fred's official baptism into a political process, and a first-hand look at Birmingham's racist system.

Fred continued to gain support by working with the Civic League, and he challenged local ministers to take a more active role in addressing the many social problems. He saw the role of the minister as God's leader of men. "Part of the problem was that the preachers were not leading," he says, "and our biblical heroes gave vivid examples of how the walls must fall when the church stands up." Fred was determined to see the walls of racism and social ills crumble.

He actively contacted various southern cities that had hired black police officers, and he sought their support for hiring black police officers in Birmingham. Several southern cities voiced their approvals and recommendations for Negro law enforcement. The Mayor of

Montgomery, Alabama was one of the first to offer his recommendations for black police officers in Birmingham. As the Birmingham Commissioners pondered Fred's demands, they indicated a willingness to compromise and accommodate Fred's "wish list." But just prior to a proposed meeting, the commissioners cited the case of Emmit Till and claimed it created an atmosphere undesirable for making a decision at the time.

At this time in history, Southern black men could not show a sexual desire (including stares, smiles, whistles, complimentary comments) or similar approval toward a white female. Not only was this type of behavior unacceptable, there were actual laws that allowed the administering of stiff penalties, even death. In Mississippi, Till, age 13, had been accused of exhibiting such behavior. He was quickly apprehended by a white mob, severely beaten, brutalized beyond recognition, thrown into the Mississippi River, where he was later found floating. Some accounts indicate he was mutilated, pulled through barbed wire, and had holes punched into his body. The alleged "crime" committed by Till was used as a basis by the Birmingham Commissioners for refusing to further consider the issue of having black police officers.

The case also focused the national spotlight on Mississippi, and the brutality against blacks that existed not only in Mississippi, but throughout the South. The unfortunate circumstances of the case provided newspapers and the media with the kind of sex appeal that sold papers and increased ratings. It basically gave the commissioners an excuse to avoid the issue. Fred had become tired and weary, but not defeated. He made it clear that the Till case was irrelevant. And Birmingham's reluctance to act in good faith only increased his desire to fight for a system of fairness and justice for all.

Clearly, Fred recognized that disagreements were inevitable. On the other hand, he was committed to handling them in a gracious manner. Grace allowed him to find some pleasure in differences, and in Birmingham, there was plenty of room for disagreements. In 1954, Fred was asked to address the Emancipation Day celebration at Sixteenth Street Baptist Church. This church, pastored by Luke Beard, would later play a vital role in the Movement and forever be a constant reminder of the sacrifice that is often paid for freedom. After his stirring speech, Fred was selected to serve as National Association for the Advancement of Colored People (NAACP) Membership Chairman, which fueled Fred's desire and hunger to bring about change. It was also 1954 when the Supreme Court ruled that segregation was unconstitutional, in *Brown v Topeka Board of Education*. This landmark decision gave Fred further incentive to lead the fight and reaffirmed his convictions that segregation was destructive and detrimental to mankind.

He was not satisfied with preaching injustice "only" to the local congregation. This was not providing solutions and resolving the problems. Thus, he let it be known that the issue had to be taken to the streets to fully dramatize the extent of the problem. As his support increased, tensions mounted. To the white populace (and some blacks) who had every intention of holding on to their racial and social dominance, Fred was a troublemaker. But, regardless of the fears and labels, Fred made his goal very clear: "The idea of the white man's superiority had to go." He knew, too, that it was not going to be a simple task. And his test of fortitude was soon to come.

Fred's campaign for black policemen continued. It included an intense campaign and circulation of a petition that gained the signatures of more than 75 ministers, 4,500 black followers, and some 100 white supporters. When the petition was presented to the City Commissioner, it made headlines in the Birmingham newspapers. This was a significant step that convinced the commissioners to hold a "good faith" meeting with Shuttlesworth's committee. His orientation in the political arena continued as he witnessed the system at work. He was amazed to see how politicians would often wait for another to vote before acting themselves. This defensive maneuver was to ensure that each one was doing the same thing. In that arena, Fred notes that he learned "that a white man often smiles when he says 'yes,' but really, he means 'hell no!'"

As Fred guided the wheel of the NAACP, he caused great concern to the established leaders of Birmingham. The NAACP had become a valuable vehicle in the fight against segregation. The U.S. Supreme Court's decision in *Brown v Topeka Board of Education*, which made it clear that segregated schools were not equal, further motivated Fred to continue. Unfortunately, his outspoken and active voice for change frightened some black ministers. But he kept reminding them that they had a moral and spiritual responsibility. But he also made it clear that, with or without their support, he would continue moving forward.

The hiring of the black policemen was a significant issue with Fred, and he refused to accept the reluctance of black clergy to provide their full support. He was convinced that the NAACP and a united church would triumph over this evil. To him, breaking down the walls of racism and hatred involved extracting one brick at a time, and this effort was a "big brick." He was certain that the results of this effort would have a tremendous impact on every other aspect of living. As he continued to distribute information and gather names on a petition for black policemen, the city commissioners realized that Fred was not about to fade into the sunset.

The power of the NAACP and the crusade of Fred and his followers continued to spread throughout Birmingham and the region. This created increased fear and panic in the hearts of the segregationists. In an effort to halt this runaway train, Alabama Governor Patterson, in May 1956, requested an injunction against the NAACP. Fred characterized the request as a "conspiracy between Southern lawmakers who were in rebellion against the Supreme Court." Fred vividly remembers the issuing of the NAACP injunction by Judge Walter B. Jones, who directed a deputy sheriff to read Fred the injunction from a document that "reached down to the floor." Fred was appalled at the decision and vowed not to abide by the ruling. He consulted with NAACP attorney Arthur Shores, who advised him that it was illegal to violate the injunction.

In fact, they were not even allowed to hold any meetings at all. Fred became distressed, but he was not to be denied the rights he felt God had bestowed upon him. Frustrated, his followers and civic leaders began turning to him for answers and direction. He assured them that he would come up with something. It wasn't long afterwards that he answered Shores with the words of John the Baptist, "You shall know the truth, and the truth shall make you free" (John 8:32 NASB). Fred organized his followers and began holding secret meetings. Although Shores was supportive, he cautioned Fred that the meetings were illegal and could result in people going to jail for violating the court injunction. Fred responded, "Well, somebody will have to go to jail then! In fact, I may be the first one to go, but the fight must go on."

As expected, the secret meetings presented considerable strain on the organization. Ministers and followers were becoming weary and frustrated. Fred, again, was expected to provide a light to a darkening night. He became increasingly disturbed, and then "one Saturday morning, I woke up and knew God had put something in my conscience." He contacted his supporters and called a Mass meeting for Tuesday night, June 5, 1956. This would be a meeting when black people would have to decide if they were ready and willing to fight for freedom. He admits that his action "at that time was like waving a red flag at a bull." Little did he know how prophetic those thoughts were. For there was certainly a bull out there, known to all as "Bull Connor."

Word of the proposed meeting wasted little time reaching city hall and the media. The media felt it was necessary to not only report this fast breaking story, but also to include the name and address of the organizer, Reverend Fred Shuttlesworth, 3191 North 29th Avenue, Birmingham, Alabama. Fred tells of a telephone call he received at 9:30 p.m. on Sunday, June 3, 1956, from Reverend Luke Beard of Sixteenth Street Baptist Church, who said, "Doc, the Lord told me to tell you to call that meeting off." The term "Doc" was often used by black ministers in respect and appreciation of those who had been called to the ministry. Fred replied, "Doc, when did the Lord start sending me messages through you? Why don't you go back to the Lord and see what He will tell you the next time!" The opposition had apparently influenced Beard to discourage Fred from going forward with his plans to officially began the Movement. It was close to midnight when Beard called again, but Fred interrupted, "Doc, tell the Lord He will have to come down Himself, with nail prints in His hands and holes in His side to get me to call it off."

Fred realized that establishing a major organization would require the skill of a well-seasoned diplomat. The segregationists were relentless in their efforts to intimidate his followers. Fred admits, "even some members in the ranks were looking for any excuse to withdraw their support." He knew he had to be an exceptional salesman to convince his followers to support his alternative to the banning of the NAACP. As he carefully plotted his strategy, he approached several of his strongest supporting ministers and outlined his plans for the creation of a new organization.

On Monday, June 4, at 2:45 p.m., in preparation for the Mass Meeting, Ministers Shuttlesworth, Nelson H. Smith, Jr., Terry L. Lane, Robert L. Alford, and George E. Pruitt, met at the Smith and Gaston Funeral Chapel, 1600 5th Avenue, N., to discuss plans, principles and resolutions to be presented at the Mass Meeting.

The discussion centered on the need for an organization to work in "our Civic interest," and the statewide implications of such an organization were mentioned by Rev. Alford. They also discussed a name for the organization. Next came the reading, discussion and the adoption of the Declaration of Principles and Resolutions to be recommended at the Mass Meeting.

Discussion centered next on various committees and the purported functioning of such committees. Suggested was a Steering Committee (to be appointed at the Mass Meeting) to appoint other committees for the organization. Each person pledged his/her all to the cause of human rights, and spoke of the need "now, for our ambitions to be realized to the point of activity."

Fred had returned to Birmingham and quickly realized that he, unlike many of the selected leaders, could not accept the social conditions of segregation imposed upon the black community. Yes, he had grown up there and had been indoctrinated to believe that it was a reality of that city. Many of the leaders were proud of their status in the community. For the most part, they had "arrived, considered themselves respected, and saw no need to cause any trouble." And although many were aware of the problems that existed, fearing possible retaliation, they were uncomfortable letting the truth be known. Thankfully, Fred was uncomfortable keeping the truth concealed.

He was mindful that exposure to anything has its risks and can be painful. Fred is a living witness that liberty often requires sacrifice, but freedom is always worth fighting for. He proclaimed, "If Jesus stood for anything, then segregation had to be wrong."

And to the dismay of the segregationists, young Fred returned to a situation that had no desire to reveal its true identity. He understood the fears of the day. Although he was lacking experience, he more than compensated for it with his vision, bravery, vigor and pure guts. His many talents and his aggressive style, while frightening to the segregationists, presented a different kind of threat to many of the well-established black leaders.

And on the night of June 5, 1956, his leadership became more evident. By the beginning of the Mass Meeting, "there were so many people, you could not get to the church." Fred aroused the audience with his stirring messages that opposed segregation and the evil of the system. The basic idea behind the meeting was to charter another organization to take the place of the banned NAACP. As Fred read a statement of principles for the proposed organization, he was bitterly challenged by Reverend J. L. Ware, G. W. McMurray and Reverend M. W. Whitt, who were greatly recognized and respected in Birmingham. Whitt denounced the thought of such an organization and argued, "You are going to get someone killed." Fred recalls, "I had given the crowd a 'rip roaring' speech, and they did not want to hear what Whitt had to say." On the other hand, Fred recognized this as an opportunity to further his status with the audience and silence his critics by impressing upon the audience that Whitt had the right to speak. So, he responded to Whitt, "Doctor, you have three minutes."

Well, Whitt spoke his three minutes and tried desperately to convince the crowd that another organization was not needed. He and Fred debated the issue briefly, and Fred, the presiding official, called upon his followers to render their verdict. Fred not only won a major victory, but seized this opportunity to further impress upon his followers that primary consideration should be given to measures that would meet non-violent objectives. To ensure that his followers were committed in their decision, Fred gave them opportunities to vote on the issue three times. Each time, the vote was overwhelming to organize.

That meeting gave birth to the Alabama Christian Movement for Human Rights (ACMHR). The objectives of the ACMHR are best summarized by Fred Shuttlesworth in a subsequent newsletter:

"Our aims and objectives are exactly the same as when we began traveling together this dangerous and uncharted road four years ago: that is, the full rights and privileges guaranteed under the Constitution of the United States to all citizens without regard to color, creed, or economic status. We take serious exceptions to any law, tradition, or custom, which sanctions the thought or practice that 'To be white is to be right,' and that the color of a man's skin is more important than his character.

"This organization stands for the full and unrestricted use of all public facilities by all, the public – the parks, the playgrounds, the schools, buses, waiting rooms, and housing. Because we stand for these things, we enjoy no blessings nor favor from the Press, City and State Officials, nor from those in the Klan and Citizens Councils.

Shuttlesworth (right) and supporters, after establishing the ACMHR. (Courtesy of Birmingham Post-Herald, © 1999.)

THE ORIGINAL DECLARATION OF PRINCIPLES

Mass Meeting On Civil Interest   Tuesday Night, June 5, 1956

CALLED BY THE FOLLOWING MINISTERS:
F. L. SHUTTLESWORTH, N. H. SMITH, JR., T. L. LANE, R. L. ALFORD AND G. E. PRUITT.

PROCEEDINGS OF THE COMMITTEE ON RESOLUTIONS:

The Committee of 11 Ministers and Laymen met June 4th, 2:45 P. M. in the Smith and Gaston Funeral Chapel, 1600 5th Ave., N., to discuss plans, Principles and Resolutions to be presented to the Mass meeting. Rev. F. L. Shuttlesworth, presided.

The discussion centered on the need of an organization to work in our Civic interest, and the State-Wide implications of such an organization was mentioned by Rev. Alford. Also discussed, was the name by which such an organization should be known. Next came the reading and discussion, and the adoption of a Declaration of Principles and Resolutions to be recommended to the Mass Meeting.

Discussion centered next on various committees, and the purported functioning of such Committees. Suggested was a Steering Committee (to be appointed in the Mass Meeting) to appoint other Committees for the organization. Each person pledged his and her all to the **Cause of Human Rights**, and spoke of the need now for our ambitions to be realized to the point of activity. The Committees makes the following recommendations:

1. That this Mass Meeting form an Organization under the name of **"THE ALABAMA CHRISTIAN MOVEMENT FOR HUMAN RIGHTS."**

2. That the following be adopted as a Declaration of Principles by the Organization:

(A) As free and independent citizens of the United States of America, and the State of Alabama, we express publicly our determination to press forward persistently for freedom and Democracy, and the removal from our society any forms of Second Class Citizenship.

(B) We are not echoing the will or sentiments of outsiders; but our own convictions and will to be free, so help us God. We will not become Rabblerousers; but will be sober, firm, peaceful, and resolute, within the Framework of Goodwill.

(C) We believe in our Courts and in Justice administered by our Courts; but we now point out to the Nation's conscience a strange paradox: One State District Court Judge can rule, and immediately it is obeyed over the entire State—even is questioned or disagreed with: But even a unanimous Decision by 9 Judges of the U. S. Supreme Court (set us by the constitution to be the Highest and Final Court), and Rulings by Federal Judges, representing the whole United States of America, are not only questioned and disagreed with, but Openly Flaunted, Disregarded, and Totally Ignored.

(D) We believe in State's Rights; but we believe that any "FIRST RIGHTS" is "HUMAN RIGHTS." And the first right of a State is to Protect Human Rights, and to guarantee to each of its Citizens the same Rights and Privileges.

(E) We heartily concur in and endorse the Rulings of the Federal Judiciary that all public facilities belong to and should be open to all on the same and equal terms; and we Hope, Trust, and Pray that efforts to commence should be begun by our Officials in the Spirit of Brotherhood and Goodwill; without the necessity of Lawsuits having to be filed.

(F) We most highly commend the activities of the Officials and Citizens everywhere for the efforts made for CIVIL RIGHTS, and we thank God for them. But especially do we applaud Negroes in Montgomery, Ala., and Tallahassee, Fla. for conducting themselves in the struggle so valiantly, and without rancor, hate, and smear, and above all without violence.

ORIGINAL DECLARATION OF PRINCIPLES (Continued)

(G) As to "Gradualism", we hold that it means to move forward, slowly maybe, but surely: not vascillation, procrastination, or evasion; and the hastily enacted laws and enflamed statements of public Officials do not lead us to embrace "Gradualism". We want a beginning NOW! **We have already waited 100 years!**

(H) We Negroes shall never become enemies of the White People: We are all Americans; but America was born in the struggle for Freedom from Tyranny and

Oppression. We shall never bomb any homes or lynch any persons; but we must, because of History and the future, march to Complete Freedom—with unbowed heads, praying hearts, and an unyielding determination. And we seek Guidance from our Heavenly Father; and from all men, Goodwill and understanding.

3. That a Steering Committee be appointed in this Mass Meeting to appoint the following other Committees: Finance, Education, Recreation, Transportation, Police Protection, Civil Rights, Jobs, Voting and Registration, Housing and Youth.

4. That this Mass Meeting go on record as unanimously supporting and applauding the efforts of Birmingham Negroes to form a Federal Loan Association in Birmingham.

5. That this Mass Meeting upon adjournment, will do so to meet Monday, June 11th, 7:00 o'clock, at the New Pilgrim Baptist Church, 903 South 6th Avenue, Birmingham, Alabama.

COMMITTEE: Revs. F. L. Shuttlesworth, N. H. Smith, Jr., R. L. Alford, C. L. Vincent, C. H. George, Atty. Oscar W. Adams, Mrs. Lucinda Robey, C. J. Evans, G. C. Gissentanner, Mr. Lewis Willie, and others.

This Organization is currently affiliated with the SOUTHERN CHRISTIAN LEADERSHIP CONFERENCE of Atlanta, Georgia.

MONDAY NIGHT MASS MEETING

THIS MEETING WAS HELD AT 17th STREET A. O. H. CHURCH, MAY 9, 1960, BISHOP JASPER ROBY, PASTOR

"We are rather hated and scorned for believing in Freedom in the Land of the Free. But we do not propose to match their envy and scorn; we choose rather to love them, pray for them, and be devoted to the brighter day for all. America needs groups like ours to exalt human dignity without reservation. Birmingham needs this Movement now more than it needs the coal and iron for which it is called 'magic.'

"For while Birmingham majors in coal, iron, and steel, the whole world knows that it minors – and drags the very bottom – in racial progress. No resource is as great and valuable as a human being; no development is more necessary than that which enhances equal opportunity, frees the human mind, and exalts the human spirit. The Movement is committed to the proposition that none is free until all are free."

The establishment of the ACMHR focused on Birmingham as the center for the Movement against segregation and for civil rights. With Fred Shuttlesworth as President and Nelson H. Smith, Jr., Secretary, they began meeting every Monday night to address issues and chart out their course of action. As they marched forward, they continued their appeal to the City Commissioners with concerns including, but not limited to, desegregation of buses, parks and public facilities, eating establishments, the hiring of black policemen and the cessation of police abuse.

Reverend Shuttlesworth and followers attending a meeting and pondering the difficult task before them. (Courtesy of Birmingham Post-Herald © 1999.)

CHAPTER 6
THE ALABAMA CHRISTIAN MOVEMENT FOR HUMAN RIGHTS: A TEST OF ENDURANCE

The ACMHR quickly established itself as a viable force in the struggle against segregation and the fight for civil rights. With Fred's continued encouragement and tenacious spirit, the organization continued to meet every Monday night. The Rosa Parks case in Montgomery had gained national attention and was being considered by the Supreme Court. The Birmingham Movement was anxiously awaiting the outcome of this case, which Fred and his followers would have to consider as they planned their future strategies.

In Birmingham, it was common practice for black Baptist churches to hold daytime Christmas Eve services. On December 24, 1956, Bethel Baptist Church was no exception, and held its church service as planned. The memory of that day and subsequent days remain vivid in Fred's mind. "I remember preaching that day and saying 'any day or night now, the Ku Klux Klan may throw dynamite into my house.'" Fred and his family had repeatedly received threatening telephone calls. In fact, the threats had become a way of life. And although Fred down played possible physical violence against him and his family, he remained aware that his life was in jeopardy.

On December 25, 1956, Fred and his family were visited by Deacon Charlie Robinson and his wife, Naomi, who had made it a normal practice to share Christmas night with their Pastor and his family. Fred and his family resided in the parsonage, which was located adjacent to the church. Fred, tired and exhausted from a demanding schedule, was lying in bed, as Charlie sat nearby. They were discussing and planning strategies to be used in future ACMHR meetings. The ACMHR had been scheduled to meet on the previous night, December 24, but because of the holiday, the meeting was rescheduled. However, Fred and his followers discretely pledged to hold a mass gathering on December 26 to begin riding city buses in spite of the segregation laws. The plans of Fred's civil disobedience had leaked to the press, and segregationists were furious with Fred's reluctance to back down. Thus, at approximately 9:45 p.m., as Fred and Charlie talked, some 16 sticks of dynamite, which had been placed below Fred's bedroom window, exploded and demolished the parsonage.

The powerful explosion collapsed the walls and structure of the parsonage and created a crater in the floor underneath Fred's bed. Fred, retaining his sense of humor, now laughs, "The mattress springs were blown out of the mattress, and they have not been seen since." Why did Fred survive such a deadly nightmare? Maybe the answer can be found in the words of Rosa Walker, who stated, "God saved him to lead the fight." Fred's wife and family, along with Charlie's wife, were in another part of the house and escaped through the rear door. His daughter Ruby sustained cuts on her hand, while Fred Jr. suffered injuries to his head. Charlie, sitting near the bed, suffered minor cuts and scratches, and he too escaped through the back door. The police responded almost immediately, along with hundreds of Fred's followers.

As Fred lay somewhat buried underneath the fallen rubble, he recalls hearing many voices of anger and concern. "They thought I was dead. People were trying to get in and police were trying to keep them out. At one point, Charlie came part way back into the house through the rear," he says. "I told him to get out because the rest of the house may fall. And I told him that I would be out as soon as I could put on my pants." A short time later, Fred was able to crawl from underneath the debris, put on his pants, and stroll out of the house as if nothing had happened. Not only was the crowd amazed to see him, they were shocked to see he barely had a scratch on him.

Immediately after crawling outside, he saw a policeman in a confrontation with a young black youth. The policeman was being rough, using profane and abusive language with the crowd in an attempt to get them away from the house. The youth, like many, was angry and excited, and did not approve of the policeman's methods. Fred observed that the youth was holding a knife in his hand in a "cuffed" position. The policeman, seeing the knife, began to grab his weapon, at which time the youth said, "If you do, I'll cut your damn throat." Fred quickly stepped in and took control of the situation to prevent further escalation. "I told the youth to put his knife away. I told the officer that the people were excited, and he needed to control himself just like they needed to control themselves."

He was approached by another officer who said, "Reverend, I am so sorry. I know these people, and I didn't think that they would go this far. But I'll tell you what I would do if I was you. I would be out of town as quick as I could." Fred replied, "Officer, you ain't me. So you go back and tell your friends, if the Lord can keep me though all of this, the war is only just beginning, and I'll be around for the duration." Fred recounts sitting in the police car, waiting to be transported to the hospital for an examination, when his six-year-old daughter, Carolyn, appeared in the door, sucking her finger. She stared at Fred, crawled up onto his lap and whispered, "They can't kill us, can they Daddy?" Fred replied, "No darling, they can't kill hope."

With little doubt, Birmingham had become the stronghold of segregation. And it was also obvious that Bethel Baptist Church and Reverend Shuttlesworth had officially become targets for racist retali-

ation. And although the police responded to this near fatal tragedy, many apparently knew that the bombing would take place. Bull Connor, Public Safety Commissioner, even commented that Shuttlesworth knew his house was going to be bombed, and that Fred was only searching for publicity. Connor challenged Fred to take a lie-detector test, but backed off when Fred agreed under the condition that Connor also take the test. Of course, one would have to believe that Fred invited guests to his home, put on his pajamas, and got into bed to await his possible fate. The bombing did little to cause Fred to retreat. In fact, the bomb may have been beneficial to the cause. His followers grew stronger in their belief that "nothing was impossible for God." Church members appealed to the good hearts of the Birmingham community for contributions and were able to immediately rebuild the parsonage.

On Friday morning, December 26th, the day following the bombing of his residence and against the wishes of his church members, Fred dispatched his followers for the previously planned riding of the buses. Fred had forewarned the city, "if you don't volunteer to let us ride, we are going to ride anyway." But Fred was concerned that the publicity would hinder him from being able to complete the rides without being disrupted by the police. Fred was also aware that Bull Connor had additional people in power who vowed to continue segregation, including Coloned Albert Lingo, State Director of Public Safety. Fred

The home of Shuttlesworth, after being bombed with 16 sticks of dynamite on December 25, 1956, by the KKK. (Courtesy of The Birmingham News Company © 1999.)

recalled how these "Law and Order" forces assigned extra police not for their protection, but to prevent the rides from taking place.

Fred prepared for this possible disruption by arranging for the riders to arrive at bus stops from different locations to avoid being detected by the media. He also instructed the riders not to sit next to another black passenger, because it would leave a seat open for white bus passengers. His plan worked to perfection. The press and the police were caught totally by surprise. To the dismay of the city, more than 250 blacks were able to ride in all areas of the city. The participation of Shuttlesworth in the ride was limited because his daughter, Patricia, was a patient at University Hospital. Although a couple dozen riders were arrested, many rode for the mere pleasure of riding. Shuttlesworth had again shown his willingness to fight segregation to the bitter end.

As Fred and his followers marched onward, a string of arrests, lawsuits, and court battles followed. It was common for Fred to file a lawsuit whenever he or protesters were denied access to the same facilities as whites. There were lawsuits involving retail stores, busses, trains, and the use of public bathrooms and facilities. Sadly, Fred had to constantly endure the mental and physical pain and discomforts of harassment and humiliation. Although he fought the constant battles of racial hatred, he was aware that there were a few concerned and supportive white people in Birmingham.

Reverend Lamar Weaver, who was acquainted with President Harry S. Truman, was one such white supporter who gained the respect and admiration of Fred and his followers. On one occasion, in 1957, Weaver arranged for Fred to meet with Truman during one of Truman's train stops in Birmingham. "You must understand that the fact that Truman met with me was significant at the time," he says. It was indeed a time when a man like Truman would not risk his reputation and image by allowing himself to be associated with the civil rights struggle and Birmingham's Movement. Fred treasures a photograph of this historic and significant meeting.

Fred recalls that in March 1957, he and his wife entered the local train station in defiance of the segregation ordinance. To enter the station, passengers and would-be passengers were required to pur-

BETHEL BAPTIST CHURCH REHABILITATION FUND

3191 NORTH 29th AVENUE

P. O. BOX 685   BIRMINGHAM, ALABAMA

THE REVEREND F. L. SHUTTLESWORTH, Minister

BOMB DEMOLISHED PARSONAGE AND DAMAGED CHURCH BUILDING

3191 North 29th Ave.
Birmingham, Alabama

Dear Friend:

At 9:45 P. M. on Christmas night, 1956, the Parsonage of the Bethel Baptist Church (See photo above) was completely destroyed by a dynamite bomb and the church was considerably damaged. It was only by a miracle of Grace that the Minister and his family were preserved alive.

This incident, while abhorred by almost all citizens of Birmingham, is nevertheless a dark blot on our city's record. But mere abhorrance alone will not make atonement for a crime or unworthy deed.

We believe that many citizens of whatever persuasion, would like to share with us in the vast effort to replace the parsonage and repair the damage done to the church of God. We feel that most men are sympathetic at heart and charitable in disposition.

Any gift which you feel led to give will be deeply appreciated by us, and applied directly to the job of reconstruction.

It will be greatly appreciated if you will pass the word on to any of your friends of like mind.

Contributions may be sent to THE BETHEL BAPTIST CHURCH REHABILITATION FUND, P. O. BOX 685, or to the Church address, 3191 North 29th Avenue, Birmingham, Alabama.

Sincerely yours,
BETHEL BAPTIST CHURCH

Rev. F. L. Shuttlesworth, Minister

William Thornton, Secretary
Charlie Watson, Treasurer

Newsletter issued by ACMHR following the bombing of Reverend Shuttlesworth's church and church parsonage on December 25, 1956.

Shuttlesworth and followers riding the city buses following the bombing of his home, December 26, 1956. (Courtesy of Birmingham Post-Herald © 1999.)

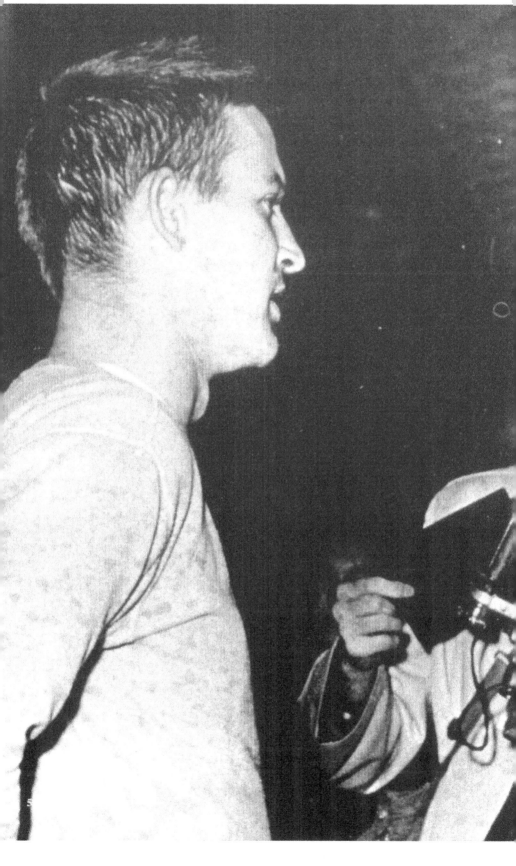

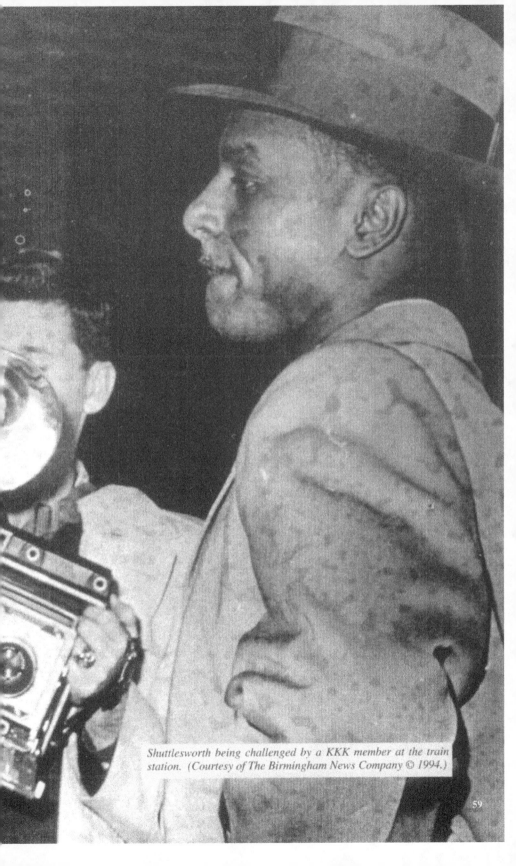

Shuttlesworth being challenged by a KKK member at the train station. (Courtesy of The Birmingham News Company © 1994.)

chase a ticket. Fred had made it known that he would be riding the train on this particular day, but found the station surrounded by an angry mob that prevented Fred and Ruby from entering the front door. So, they followed the police through a side door and entered a waiting area until the police could force the mob out of the terminal. Weaver, who was an avid supporter, stopped in the station to give Fred moral support.

Unfortunately, Weaver did not have a train ticket and was not authorized to enter the station. The policeman, on duty to keep an eye on Fred, forced Weaver back out into the angry mob, which attacked and badly beat Weaver. According to Fred, Weaver was able to make his way back into his car, which was being attacked and severely damaged. As Weaver sped away in his vehicle to avoid the violent attack, he was stopped by a police officer, cited for running a traffic light, and ordered by a judge to pay a $10 fine.

As the Movement continued its fight for equality, Fred was aware of the difficulty of the task. But he also knew that his followers were great people. History had shown that black people had often risen to meet difficult challenges. Fred realized there were those in the world who were busy building towers with highest hopes of gaining fame and making a name for themselves.

Fred was more concerned about serving God and the needs of His people. He could not accomplish that without purifying a city and saving souls. Fred reasoned that, "even segregationists can be saved." He continued to remain optimistic for a change in Police Commissioner Bull Connor, who made it clear that he did not accept black people as his equal. That kind of thinking was the crux of the problem. So Fred, as a servant of Christ, went forward, committed that he would "not be overcome by evil, but overcome evil with good" (Romans 12:21 NASB).

In 1954, the Supreme Court, in *Brown v Topeka Board of Education*, ruled that segregation in public schools was not equal education, and it would not be tolerated. Apparently, the lines of communication were not open to many cities around the country, including Birmingham. This was more than evident in 1957, when black children were still not allowed to take advantage of this decision from the high court.

Shuttlesworth and his wife, Ruby, at the train station. (Courtesy of Birminham Post-Herald © 1999.)

Fred was concerned with the total development of all black people, including their access to the educational system. In addition to his daughter Carolyn, he and Ruby were proud parents of three other children, Fred Jr., Patricia, and Ruby. But in Birmingham, the Police Commissioner made no secret of his thoughts of equality by constantly fighting to sustain segregation and the evils of racial hatred at all cost. However, in September 1957, Fred decided to help open those lines and convey the message of the high court. He and Ruby decided to enroll Patricia and Ruby in the all-white Phillips High School. Both of the young girls were enrolled in Parker High, the all-black School, and were required to drive past Phillips High enroute to Parker.

In an effort to ensure the safety of his children and prevent any misunderstanding, Fred notified the local school officials and the police of the scheduled enrollment plans. He sought a long time friend, J. S. Phifer, Pastor of Zion Star Baptist Church, to drive him and his family, and Nathaniel Lee, another student, to the school for registration. Phifer and Fred sat in the front, while Ruby and the children sat in the back seat. When they arrived at the school, they were immediately greeted by a hostile mob that immediately surrounded the car. The events that followed were only a minor indication of the severity of the infectious disease that had penetrated the hearts of many misguided souls. Fred sighs,

Shuttlesworth, meeting with President Harry S. Truman and Lamar Weaver. (Courtesy of the Birmingham News Company © 1994)

Shuttlesworth (right) being attacked by a mob in September 1957, during his attempt to enroll his children in Phillips High School.

"I was getting out of the car when they grabbed me and my clothing. They began kicking, punching and beating me with chains and brass knuckles. This was the first time in my life I had seen brass knuckles, and I was being beaten by one. At one point, my coat was pulled over my head, so I had to get it down so I could see. I was dragged about 20 feet while being beaten. As I struggled to get back to the car, they continued to beat me. I was able to barge into one of the attackers as I lunged forward to get back into the car. My wife, when getting out of the car, had the door pushed back on her. She recalled feeling a sharp pain in her hip, but because she was wearing a thick girdle, she did not know what it was. It was not until we arrived at the hospital did she learn that she had been stabbed with a knife."

His daughter, Ruby (Bester), now living in Cincinnati, finds it difficult to reflect on the horrible scene that followed. She experienced instant fear as they arrived at the school, and asked if they should be going there. She remembers seeing her father open the door, and then being "pulled from the car and beaten with chains." It is an awful memory for her. She attempted to get out of the car, but someone pushed the door shut on her ankle, which forced her to retreat into the vehicle. That may have just saved her life, or at least prevented serious injury. "A local TV anchorman who was there to film the event was even beaten with the chains," she says.

Shuttlesworth asking for non-violence, after being released from the hospital in September 1957. (Courtesy of The Birmingham News Company © 1999.)

The mere image of the scene and the physical punishment endured by Fred and his wife should be enough to awaken the consciousness of the common man and allow him to appreciate the courage and tenacity of the Shuttlesworth family. If not, then consider Fred's physical condition and appearance upon arrival at the hospital. The wounds included severely bruised ears, skin ripped from his body, severe facial bruises and disfigurement and blood flowing from his head and face. These were major conditions, which probably would have left other men permanently impaired, in a coma, or worse.

Doctors were stunned when a complete physical examination revealed that Fred, after having suffered this brutal beating and conditions that should have caused shock, or some degree of trauma, still had a normal pulse rate and remained in high spirits. It was evident that Fred was not a common man. And through it all, Fred never lost his sense of humor. Even the medical staff was baffled at his optimism. When a doctor commented on his positive attitude, Fred let it be known that God had a job that needed to be done, and he had been chosen to get it done. Maybe that is why Bull Connor referred to Reverend Fred Shuttlesworth as the primary social problem in all of Birmingham.

Truly, God prepared Fred for a task that no one had attempted, and might not have attempted. The Movement had already cost him severe pain and discomfort, and almost his life, but it never cost him his faith. Birmingham, with its hatred, racism, and bitterness, had been accurately identified as "the Johannesburg of the South." Perhaps no one was more aware of what that meant than Fred. But he was determined to see that this battle was won. Fred believed that his actions were for the glory of God. And anything that does not result in God's glory should cause every man to redirect his energy and allow God's spirit to work through him.

Even to this day, the spirit that was working in Fred does not permit him to harbor any resentment or hatred for those who inflicted so much harm upon him and others. Following his attack by the high school mob, several of the mob members were arrested. He was not angered that they were not indicted. "They were doing what they believed was right, and I was doing what I believed was right." Even

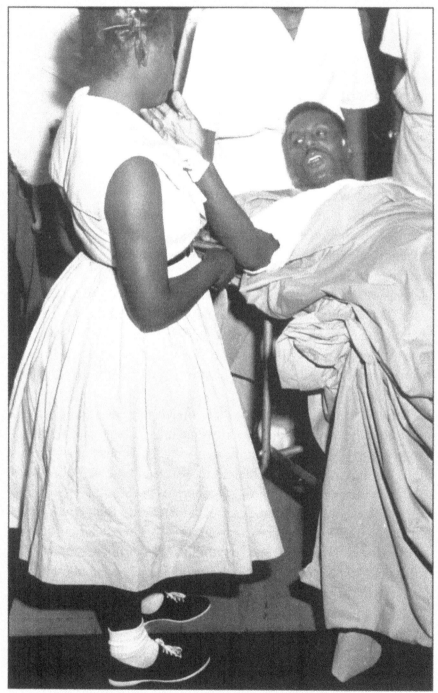

Shuttlesworth, providing comfort to his daughter, Patricia, following the beating at Phillips High School. (Courtesy of The Birmingham News Company © 1994.)

more amazing, after being released from the hospital, an angry crowd of supporters met him, perhaps expecting some type of retaliation. Reporters anxiously waited for some fast-breaking news. But anger was not in his heart. Instead, Fred calmly spoke to his followers and called for non-violence and forgiveness.

It was clear that the mere thought of Reverend Shuttlesworth angered Bull Connor. He assigned extra manpower to monitor the activities of Fred and relied upon every kind of tactic to undermine Fred's credibility and to abuse his followers. Plain-clothes officers made themselves noticeable at ACMHR meetings, actively taking notes, while attempting to intimidate those present, and followers who wanted to be present. And it was common for Fred to be arrested for the slightest indication that he was violating a law. To the satisfaction of Bull Connor, Fred became a common guest in Hotel Birmingham (jail). An arrest did not always result in actual charges. Nevertheless, the scenes became redundant: arrest Fred, disrupt and intimidate his followers, and drop the charges. These were just a few of the many nightmares of Fred's everyday living. Nightmares that motivated Fred to answer every bell ready to fight and more determined as each day passed. His determination was exemplified in the voices of demonstrators and marchers who later sang, "I ain't afraid of your jail, because I want my freedom, want my freedom, want my freedom now."

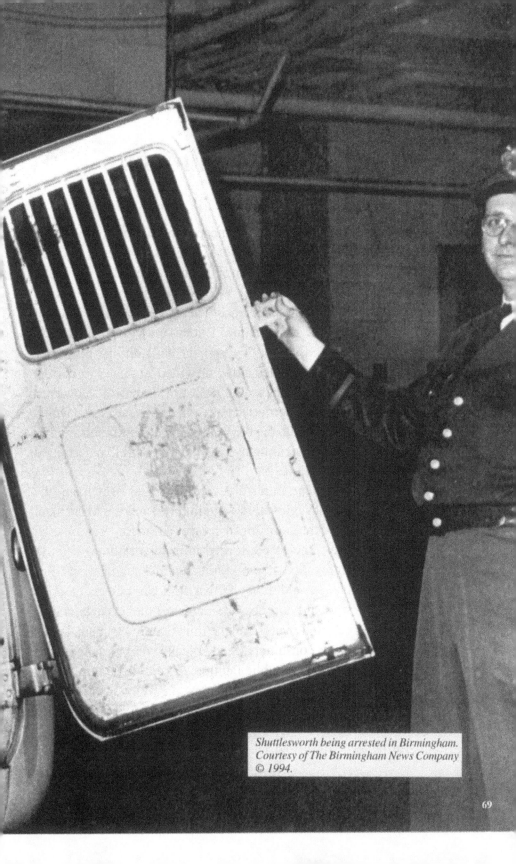

Shuttlesworth being arrested in Birmingham.
Courtesy of The Birmingham News Company
© *1994.*

CHAPTER 7
FEAR TURNS VIOLENT

The ACMHR stood proud of its success in holding its followers together, even under constant adverse conditions of threats, fear, arrest, and violence against them. The march continued in the battle against the evil laws of segregation. Efforts to pursue positive results through petitions were not sufficient. Therefore, lawsuits, another avenue, were often the course of action. Prior to the Movement, blacks were unable to seek and obtain government civil service positions. The courts, although sometimes slow, provided a means to correct this. Court action allowed blacks the right to ride buses. However, police and bus drivers were permitted to assign designated seats, which meant blacks were directed to the back. As a result, Fred filed another lawsuit, which resulted in a ruling by the Federal Court that permitted passengers to sit in any seats.

Prior to the Movement, ministers were restricted from using the pulpit to preach against segregation. Again, Fred and the Movement took action and opened the doors for such cases as the Reverend Calvin Woods' boycott case. The case afforded ministers the legal right to preach to their congregations from pulpits against segregation. For the first time, ministers could freely protest the economic genocide of black citizens. Fred and his followers increased their attack against merchants and stores, and focused on the injustices in hiring and merchandise sales to black consumers. Since blacks were not allowed to work in retail stores and use public facilities, it was difficult to verify the actual extent of racism employed against them.

Fred realized the significance of organization and support. He readily admits that the ACMHR was held together by three brave and resourceful ladies: Lola Hendricks, Julia Rainge and Georgia Price.

"They were the catalyst for the organization," he says. He knew that he could be in New York, Detroit, Los Angeles or anywhere in the country, and could depend on these three "soldiers" to organize and plan strategic action. He talks with pride about how these three ladies maintained a network of supporters in strategic locations throughout the city. His face lights up as he recalls the many times he made telephone calls to them, and with just a few hours notice, requested a Mass Meeting. These ladies were always able to bring hundreds of followers together, motivated and ready to follow him. He was convinced that his actions were being directed by the will of God.

The Movement continued to attract the attention and penetrate the souls of millions from around the world. This was not South Africa, but America, "The Land of the Free, The Home of the Brave." But the segregationists continued in their attempts to strangle the efforts of Fred and his followers. The fight began to cost both sides. As Fred strategically launched lawsuits, the city leaders became more angered by Fred's disruptive legal actions. On the other hand, Fred's army continued to endure arrest, physical and mental agony.

More so, the Movement was experiencing mounting financial hardships. Although the organization first sought progress by petition and goodwill, the filing of lawsuits became mandatory and expensive. The Movement had made it possible for blacks to apply for county and city civil service positions and stood ready to file additional legal claims. But expenditures for bonds, transcripts, court costs, and legal fees during the 1950s exceeded $50,000. And through it all, Fred found a way to motivate his followers, in spite of continued harassments designed to dampen their spirits.

One person who was very aware of the extensive cost of the Movement was Lola Hendricks of Titusville, a suburb of Birmingham. Lola was born in Birmingham, graduated from Birmingham's Booker T. Washington Business College, and was committed to working with every organization for civil rights. To this day, she continues to serve as a lifelong volunteer with many Birmingham organizations.

Throughout the South, segregation laws, also called Jim Crow laws, were strictly enforced. It wasn't until after violent confrontations in Birmingham and many other Southern cities in the 1950s and 1960s that the laws were struck down. The laws dated back to Reconstruction and were used to keep blacks from exercising the freedoms that whites enjoyed, despite the abolition of slavery. The laws touched all aspects of everyday life; where you ate, lived, worked, went to school, where you worshipped, and even where you were buried. Blacks understood that they were not to make eye contact when talking to whites. They were to step off the sidewalk into the street to let whites pass, and they were to address whites as "sir" or "ma'am." Black citizens were constantly reminded of their "second-class status."

Lola knew far too well the hardships of that day. She also knew the heart of Fred Shuttlesworth and his commitment to bring about social and economic change. She had become Fred's friend, confidant, ACMHR's Corresponding Secretary, and a catalyst of the organization. When local ministers decided to fight the laws in Birmingham, she was one of the first to step forward. Whenever a church bombing occurred, she quickly answered the call, and was always armed with pen and paper to report damages or significant events.

Lola was present during meetings and marches, and offered advice and support to Shuttlesworth and others in the Movement. Although the truth of racism can be painful to confront, Lola feels it is essential for blacks to remember their history and for whites to understand the injustices of racism. "We had decided that we were tired of second-class everything. We had no idea at that time how powerful we would become," she said.

Beginning in the 1960s, lunch counter sit-ins were favorite tactics of Fred and his followers. The sit-in activity soon spread, as black college students became more active in cities including Greensboro, Charlotte, Durham, and Winston Salem, North Carolina. They demonstrated additional civil disobedience in Rock Hill, South Carolina (birthplace of the author); Hampton, Virginia; and DeLand, Florida.

Bull Connor angrily defied any such activity in Birmingham. But Shuttlesworth actively recruited students, who were trained to enter stores and request service at lunch counters. Those who participated faced certain fines and jail sentences. For instance, Fred was arrested and convicted for civil disobedience and violating the segregation laws.

Birmingham's Recorders Judge William Conway imposed a fine of $100 plus costs and 180 days in jail, which was the common penalty imposed by the court.

During the trial, the court called students to testify, which was sufficient testimony in the conviction. Students James Gober and James P. Davis recounted how demonstrators had met in the Shuttlesworth home with Reverend Charles Billups to recruit volunteers and discuss a strategy for the lunch counter demonstrations. Once, during a sit-in attempt at a local restaurant, Shuttlesworth ordered a ham sandwich and a cup of coffee, and was charged $15. He now chuckles, "It was a good thing I didn't order a steak."

Another time, he was found guilty and fined $100 and costs, and was given another 180 days in jail for allegedly providing police with false information. The case related to Fred's request that the Birmingham Police investigate an attempted castration of James Mallory, a black youth, by several white men. Fred had apparently sent telegrams to the Police Department, the FBI, the State Attorney General, and the Highway Patrol. However, during the trial, Mallory testified he had suffered the injuries at the hands of his wife. He also testified that he had not told anyone he was attacked by white men, and he denied asking Shuttlesworth to demand an investigation. Shuttlesworth and several witnesses countered Mallory's testimony by assuring the court that Mallory had indeed requested assistance from the ACMHR. Even if the wife had inflicted the wound, which was unlikely, Shuttlesworth contended that the assailants, black or white, should not go unpunished.

Fred, in every sense, had come to realize that suffering, in some degree, is unavoidable. He had made up his mind that he was not going to give up or give in to suffering. To Fred, suffering only provided him with hidden opportunities for achievement. The kind of opportunities which caused the poet Rilke to write, "How much suffering there is to get through." It was an adopted principal that was desperately needed to nourish the weak and encourage the strong.

It was the kind of strength experienced by Viktor Frankl, a former prisoner in Hitler's concentration camp, in his quote of Nietzsche: "That which does not kill me, makes me stronger." Unknowingly,

Bull Connor and the *Birmingham News* contributed mightily in the process of making Fred stronger. *The News* generally supported the position of Bull Connor. In the columns of *The News*, Connor actively expressed opposition to Shuttlesworth and the civil rights activists. Connor, inciting racial hatred, was repeatedly published in the daily columns of *The News*.

Only when *The News* viewed Connor's behavior as a detriment to the community's image did it take a critical view of his actions. Such was the case in 1958 when three black Montgomery ministers were arrested for the mere act of visiting Birmingham. *The News* voiced strong opposition and dissatisfaction with the 1957 castration of a black man by the Ku Klux Klan. But even in that case, *The News* accused northern newspaper journalists of instigating unrest with their "ugly headlines." On the other hand, *The News* was routinely critical of Shuttlesworth and the ACMHR, and often labeled them as being "extremists" who were disruptive forces in the city.

To say the least, local businesses and politicians resented "northern" intrusion into Birmingham's problems. Charles Brooks, *The News'* political cartoonist, illustrated this widespread resentment in a 1959 cartoon. The drawing showed three monkeys, representing northern newspapers, who failed to see, hear, or speak of the evils of northern race relations, but who became wildly excited about "racial troubles in the South." Day-by-day, the troubles and injustices that existed in Birmingham and the south were exposed to all the world by northern journalists.

More than anyone else, *New York Times* reporter Harrison Salisbury forced *The News* and the entire Birmingham white community to confront the reality of racial conflict. In April 1960, the *Times* published Salisbury's profile of the city under the headline, "Fear and Hatred Grip Birmingham." Salisbury wrote,

> "Every channel of communication, every medium of mutual interest, every reasoned approach, every inch of middle ground has been fragmented by the emotional dynamite of racism, enforced by the whip, the razor, the gun, the bomb, the torch, the club, the knife, the mob, the police and many branches of the state's apparatus."

Birmingham's leaders first responded to the article with fear and hatred of Salisbury. The Chamber of Commerce charged the *Times* with making false and inflammatory statements and demanded a retraction. The three Birmingham city commissioners sued the *Times* for libel. But Salisbury's vivid imagery and absolute judgment printed in the nation's most influential newspaper put the burden of proof on Birmingham to show that it was not a city of fear and hatred. The arguments and allegations, presented in Federal Court, could not be substantiated, and the case went down to defeat. Salisbury's article can be seen as a major turning point in the city's history, and it contributed to redirecting the attitudes of the community's business and civic leaders.

In August 1960, Reverend Shuttlesworth and his followers extended their message of freedom beyond the borders of Birmingham. The law required that Negroes, when riding Greyhound and Trailways interstate buses, must move to the rear. In that year, Shuttlesworth and his followers, determined not to be denied their God-given rights, set their sights on this law as the next wall that had to be removed. By this time, Fred's children had become active participants in the Movement.

Fred Jr., who now resides in Cincinnati, applauds his father for his leadership during these turbulent times. "Daddy always made sure that he protected us, and our parents tried to keep us from being directly involved so we couldn't get hurt." During 1960, Fred Jr. recalls how several groups in Birmingham attempted to bridge the gap between the races by holding an interracial summer camp. Camp Highlander, at Monteagle, Tennessee, consisted of children from all racial, cultural, and religious groups from all over the world, who were brought together for a six-week period. Fred Jr., Patricia, and Ruby gladly participated in this experience that included, "daily games, sports, songs, and just regular fun," says Fred Jr. It was especially beneficial for Fred Jr. because, "never, ever had I been in contact with a white person, except in a store," he explains. The objective was for the youth to experience living and growing up in a diverse group.

The venture was apparently successful. Fred and his sisters left the camp feeling much better about themselves and what they had to offer society. Patricia had a memorable experience with an atheist that proved to be crucial in her understanding that everyone does not believe in God. At the conclusion of their six weeks, the group boarded a Greyhound Bus and began their journey back to Birmingham. The bus was so crowded, Fred and his sisters were required to stand in the aisle, about half-way to the rear. During the trip, as the young people were laughing and recounting their experiences at the camp, the white bus driver became annoyed and ordered them to the rear of the bus.

According to Fred Jr., "We had learned through our father and the Movement, that we did not have to move to the rear of the bus." Well, apparently, the bus driver had learned differently. At approximately 10 p.m., when the bus arrived in Gadsden, Alabama, the driver stopped and called the police, who arrested the Shuttlesworth youth. They were immediately taken to the Gadsden City Jail, where the police began asking questions. When an officer approached Patricia, she was too hoarse from all the singing and excitement of the camp and could not speak. The police officer accused Patricia of refusing to speak up, and "slapped her in the face." Fred Jr., having witnessed the unjust attack on his sister, immediately responded to her rescue, but the officer "grabbed me around my neck and began choking me," he said.

Patricia, age 16, telephoned her father to report the arrest. The two girls were placed in jail cells together, and Fred Jr. was placed in a cell on a different floor. The girls, well-knowing the harm and/or death often inflicted on black men, feared the worst for their brother. Due to their separation, Fred Jr. was fearful that violence was being inflicted on his sisters. To ease the worrying and painful thoughts, he began singing some of the songs he had learned in the summer camp. What he did not realize was that his sisters could hear him singing, which provided them with assurance that he was all right.

Shuttlesworth immediately obtained "bail bonds" to use for their release, and sought several friends to accompany him to Gadsden. Upon arrival in Gadsden, the police met his convoy on the outskirts of the city limits. Fred, after being accused of "bringing an army to Gadsden," informed the police that he enjoyed traveling with company. However, to avoid additional confrontations, Fred sent his escorts, except James Armstrong, back to Birmingham. After arriving at the police station, his bonds were refused by the officer on duty who pointed out that the documents were "Birmingham Bonds." Fred's plea for the release of his children fell on deaf ears, and he informed the police that he and Armstrong would be spending the night in a local motel. As they drove to the motel, a police vehicle closely followed. This encouraged Fred to use every precaution and obey all traffic laws to avoid being arrested himself.

The following day, Shuttlesworth was successful in obtaining acceptable bonds from a Gadsden medical doctor. But his return to the local jail, and subsequent court hearings, were not without further obstacles. The court alleged that the Shuttlesworth family did not provide proper parental supervision and ruled that the children were delinquents, which meant they would be placed in court custody. However, Fred refused to accept the judgment, and he forced the court to hold additional hearings. This bold action by Fred resulted in the later dismissal of the case without further action.

In the meantime, according to Fred, Shores, ACMHR attorney, insisted on expenses beyond the means of the ACMHR. The expenses for bonds, court costs, and fees were staggering. And in Fred's opinion, "the Birmingham lawyers had done the bare minimum in representing ACMHR cases." Fred sensed that the lawyers felt little concern for the passing of time and the continued sacrifice being made by the many warriors directly involved in the daily battles. Fred notes, "the attorneys needed to realize we were in a fight."

Regardless, discontent with legal representation opened the door for Len Holt, a young black attorney from Virginia, who took up the fight with Fred. Whenever Fred and the ACMHR were involved in a court hearing, the presiding judge, in attempting to discourage Holt, scheduled several court dates. After Holt had traveled all the way from Virginia, he would cancel the hearings.

But young Holt, from the firm of Jordan, Gall and Holt, was not easily discouraged. He had been characterized as radical, but radicals are often needed to champion a cause, and this in everyway was a "cause." Holt was more than reasonable in his charges. While handling several cases in Gadsden, he was required to make numerous trips from Virginia. He only charged a meager $500 in comparison with local lawyers, who according to Fred, would have charged over $25,000.

By 1961, the Movement had all the ingredients of a powder keg just waiting for the lighting of the fuse. As expected, in May, the fuse was ignited. The Congress of Racial Equality (CORE), a national civil rights organization which had recently organized and joined the many ongoing battles, began testing a desegregation order directing desegregation of interstate buses. CORE, having coordinated its plans with Shuttlesworth and the ACMHR, sent an integrated group of students on a bus tour of the South to determine if the South was in compliance. The students, called the "Freedom Riders," would leave an indelible mark on the conscience of not only the South, but of the nation. One group, arriving in Anniston, Alabama, had their bus fire bombed, and were severely beaten by an angry mob. Another group arrived at Birmingham's Trailways bus station on Mother's Day morning, May 14, and was immediately attacked by a mob composed partly of Ku Klux Klansmen. The powder key had exploded and revealed again the viciousness of hatred and segregation.

And so, on May 15, 1961, even *The News* had to recognize and admit to a cancer that had been rapidly eating away at the city of Birmingham. The infectious issues and circumstances forced an editorial by Vincent Townsend that read:

"Sunday, May 14, was a day which ought to be burned into Birmingham's conscience. Fear and hatred did stalk Birmingham's streets yesterday. Fear and hatred stalked the sidewalks around the Greyhound bus terminal directly across the street from Birmingham City Hall. Fear and hatred rode around in a dozen or more automobiles loaded with men, some of whom may have been from Birmingham, others of whom positively were from other counties. License plates gave them away. But yesterday, hoodlums took over a section of Birmingham. They clustered in small groups, they drove around in cars, they all but swaggered. They were not afraid, they were sure of themselves, they knew about the 'freedom riders' and the buses they were supposed to come in on, and they had the place staked out – both the Greyhound bus terminal and, a bit more than two blocks away, the Trailways bus terminal. Others knew this situation existed. Commissioner Eugene Connor, on duty at City Hall, was well aware of the situation. Klansmen or other hoodlums were ready to create trouble."

The fact that David Lowe, producer of *CBS Reports*, a national network program, and Howard K. Smith, a well-known national television reporter, were in Birmingham to record the events did not deter the violent actions of the mob. Nor did it encourage the police to take appropriate action. These facts prompted *The News* to add,

"In trying to defend the South they invited every imaginable weapon to be trained against us. And the police of Birmingham did not stop the trouble that did develop. *The Birmingham News* wonders why. The police knew what was up – the presumed two buses, one a Greyhound, one a Trailways, carrying the 'freedom riders' from Anniston where they already had run into trouble – with a Molotov cocktail type of bomb being tossed into one of the buses. At the Trailways Terminal yesterday afternoon, with the conditions above prevailing, a bus pulled in, and all but in an instant, a Negro was being beaten, his trousers almost torn off, a white man being beaten by a hoodlum who repeatedly smashed his face with the fist."

Not even the news media was exempt from attack. The *News* continued,

"A *Birmingham Post-Herald* photographer was being pummeled by a group of white men, one of whom had a heavy instrument in a brown paper bag. The photographer was repeatedly struck, and our own witnesses saw this brutal encounter. He was beaten to the concrete behind the Trailways Terminal, his head striking with a sickening thud. One of the hoodlums repeatedly kicked him in the ribs. But this wasn't all. These bums saw other photographers – two from the *Birmingham News*. They mobbed these newsmen and, with a threat which from our own witnesses might very well have meant death if a wrong move were made, tore out the film from two *News* cameras. But this wasn't all, either. Within minutes a radio-television newsman, parked in a plainly-marked TV station wagon, right by the Birmingham Post Office, was attacked – perhaps by the same thugs who had pipe-whipped and kicked a *Post-Herald* photographer, beaten a Negro and another white man, and who had ripped out the *Birmingham News* camera's film which had taken shots of what was happening, had been happening – films to show the people of Birmingham and anyone else what was going on."

The precise location of these conditions, on this day, was on 19th Street between the Trailways terminal at Fourth Avenue and the Greyhound Terminal at Seventh Avenue. The thugs, infested with racist hatred and fear, did what they had set out to do, and up to this time had gotten away with it. Shuttlesworth, who continued to make himself a target for segregationists, met the bus only to be arrested for "interfering with police." The charge was later overturned by the U. S. Supreme Court. It was a rotten day for the City of Birmingham, for the State of Alabama, and for the United States. *The News* had supported Eugene Connor for police commissioner before the first primary, and Connor swept into office handily after proclaiming that the City of Birmingham would not tolerate violence, disorder, and the breaking of law. But on this day, *The Birmingham News* charged,

"The very men who did these beatings, who smashed to the concrete and kicked and battered a Post-Herald photographer, who ripped film from two cameras of *The News*, who in broad daylight bashed in two windows of a radio-

TV news station wagon, up to an hour or more later were plainly visible, still carrying on their vicious patrol in the whole area and particularly in the Greyhound bus terminal area."

Once again, Birmingham displayed its reputation as being the darkest spot on the American continent, and maybe the hardest. Segregationists had long proclaimed around the world that the "Negro is satisfied." But now, people throughout the country were asking the questions: "Why the push by Negroes to vote? Why the sit-ins, stand-ins, Freedom Rides and relentless bombings? Why was there a day of violent attacks on defenseless people in Birmingham on May 14, 1961?" The truth was simple, the Negro had never been satisfied! But the fight continued to be costly, due in part to the city officials, police, local and state courts who were arrayed against justice and freedom for the negro. But Shuttlesworth and his followers boldly sounded their voices, "We shall overcome, because the Lord will see us through!"

In May 1961, a week after the "freedom riders" arrived in Birmingham and met a violent reception, an army of federal marshals headed for Alabama. Their arrival prompted a front page editorial in the Sunday edition of *The News*:

"We, the people, asked for Federal action and we got Federal action.

We, the people – the same people who said, in various degrees, 'they got what they deserved.'

We, the people, who let our government, our police commissioner, our elected and appointed officials, state, county and municipal, believe that we did not mean it when we said that we wanted law and order.

We, the people, let the governor of the great state of Alabama, John Patterson, talk for months in a manner that could easily say to the violent, the intemperate, the 'interested citizens' (as the governor called them Saturday) that they were free to do as they pleased when it came to the 'hated' integrationist.

We, the people – the newspaper people, the lawyers, the bankers, the executives, the labor leaders, the clergy and the average householders, workers and businessmen – permitted a condition to arise that let intolerance and brutality take over in Anniston, Birmingham and Montgomery. You have read some of the letters...signed by responsible people...that said that 'they got what they deserved.'

We, the people, let a reporter-photographer for the *Birmingham Post-Herald* 'get what he deserved.'

We, the people, let radio-television reporter Chancy Lake 'get what he deserved.'

We, the people, let the radio, television and newspaper people – whose principle sin seemed to be that they wanted to protect freedom of information so that the public in general might know the things that were being done in their name in Anniston, Montgomery and Birmingham –'get what they deserved.'

We, the people, have let gangs of vicious men ride this state now for months. They have been riding in Tuscaloosa, Talledega, in Sylacauga, in a dozen other fine towns and communities.

We, the people, have let the men whom Governor Patterson Saturday termed 'interested citizens' ride the highways and the streets, 'interested citizens' who by their very attitudes have threatened the peace and happiness of the state. They have been, and are today, men who take the law and order in their own hands.

We, the people, have let our police officers and officials be shamed by these men, shamed because we have not demanded, of our governor, our officials, whether they be public safety commissioners or sheriffs and police chiefs, that these men be stopped, be investigated, be jailed for their plots and plans against us, the people.

So today, another Sunday, this time May 21, an army of United States Marshals is marching on Alabama.

Shuttlesworth being arrested in Birmingham, AL, during the Freedom Rides, 1961. (Courtesy of the Birmingham News Company © 1994.)

They are coming because we did not do our duty to ourselves and our proud state.

These Federal officers will be able to see that the so-called 'freedom riders' – the stupid zealots who came to provoke us into acts that would bring about such Federal action – ride the bus, integrate the bus station lunchrooms and waiting rooms, privileges given them already by federal court edict.

And what are the people of Alabama going to do now?

Are they going to counsel together, go into action, marshal the leadership of the press, the pulpit, the labor unions, industrial management, to demand of their police, their public officials, yes their governor, that the law of the land be maintained?

Are they going to marshal their spiritual strength against hatred?

Are they going to demand that the force of the law be exerted fully against race agitating visitors and 'interested citizens,' those who use the knife, the lead pipe and the gang attack to bring about a condition that takes the due process of law out of the hands of good Alabamians and put it in the hands of federal enforcement agencies?

We, the people, asked for it. As we wail in our anguish, let us not forget it."
Published May 21, 1961

Birmingham had inherited the Freedom Riders. And although the plans for the rides originated in Washington, D.C., Shuttlesworth and his followers were cooperating with its overall purpose of breaking down the Freedom Barriers. Shuttlesworth and the Freedom Riders had clearly shown that Federal laws were being flagrantly violated. Unfortunately, in unveiling this ugly picture to all the world, many had to suffer, some had to die. The battlegrounds were drawn in Birmingham, but a close examination of the problems further illustrated the inhuman atrocities being inflicted on black citizens throughout the racist South.

However, the results included the awakening of a nation to the viciousness of a "free nation." In thirty days, all signs at bus and train stations previously designating "White and Colored" were removed. Restrictions of "White Only" on civil service applications were removed. Had not such demonstrations occurred, those signs would have remained indefinitely. The sad day of May 14, and many days that preceded it, were painful experiences for some whites, people of color everywhere, and for a nation that proudly proclaimed "justice and liberty for all."

But the battle was far from over. By July 1961, the Reverend Fred L. Shuttlesworth was hailed by CBS reporters as "The man most feared by Southern Racists, and the voice of the new militancy among Birmingham Negroes." One must ask, why was he labeled "militant?" His tenacity, energy and voice for change had caught the attention of the congregation of the Revelation Baptist Church in Cincinnati, Ohio. Before long, he accepted the Pastorate at Revelation. Why would Fred even consider leaving at such a difficult time? He quickly defends his decision:

"Reverend L.V. Booth of Zion Baptist Church in Cincinnati had always been a loyal supporter of civil rights. I had promised him that by 1961, I would re-locate to Cincinnati. It just happens that during that time period, Lamar Weaver, who was also a friend of the pastor of Revelation Baptist Church, was traveling to Cincinnati, and asked me to worship with him at Revelation. I agreed and traveled to Cincinnati. Unfortunately, the pastor of Revelation died. In November, I preached at Revelation on the subject of 'Consecration,' and the church immediately sought me as their pastor. I accepted, but I want you to know that I did not leave the Birmingham crisis. I preached at Revelation, but I continued to live and fight in Birmingham."

Revelation may have failed to realize that in Birmingham Fred Shuttlesworth, for the most part, was the Movement. His work was deeply ingrained in those goals. He was the heart of the massive struggle against segregation. Thus, he continued to identify and violate any segregation laws established by the city, and then challenge their validity in the courts. By 1971, Shuttlesworth had become the most litigious individual in the history of the U. S. Supreme Court, having appeared before the body eleven times in civil rights-related cases.

As Shuttlesworth challenged Bull Connor and local leaders, his voice and the torch he ignited were burning around the nation. But sadly, the local officials treated the matter as if there was little concern. National leaders were often more concerned about their political future than "doing the right thing," Fred says. Fred's tenacity and vigor had brought hundreds of college students into the city in support of his efforts. The students, black and white, had suffered, and some died for the simple rights guaranteed by the U.S. Constitution.

Although he accepted the responsibility and task of preaching at Revelation, he continued his involvement with the Movement and ACMHR by commuting weekly to Birmingham to coordinate and carry out their mandates. At the request of his other Civil Rights compatriots, he continued to serve as Secretary of the Southern Christian Leadership Conference, Atlanta, Georgia, and as Board Member of the Southern Conference Educational Fund at New Orleans, Louisiana.

Reverend Shuttlesworth exalting and encouraging his followers with one of many "rip roaring" speeches. (Photo by Danny Lyon, courtesy of Magnum Photos, Inc.)

CHAPTER 8
UNITING WITH DR. KING

Reverend Shuttlesworth assumed his pastorate position at a time when the Movement was reaching its expected climax. With his attention divided, it was difficult to respond to the needs of his new congregation in Cincinnati. They had repeatedly sought him to help fulfill their vision, and to guide them through their dark days in hope of seeing a brighter tomorrow. Shuttlesworth recognized this as an additional challenge, and felt Cincinnati was where God was directing him to go. But he had spent his life laying the foundation for change in Birmingham and throughout the world. He was now beginning to see the fruits of his labor. His hard work and sacrifice were revolutionizing not only the South, but lives throughout America. With his vision, endurance and fortitude, although slow and painful, change was taking place. During the remainder of 1961, while his family remained in Birmingham, he continued to travel from Cincinnati to Birmingham in an effort to continue the building of a new Birmingham, a new South.

During the summer of 1962, Shuttlesworth moved his family to Cincinnati, but he was unable to release his grip on Birmingham. Not only was his heart still there, he maintained a sense of mission. The Movement continued to call out his name. Birmingham needed him, and there were far too many battles to be won. The nation and the world were in need of fully realizing the plight of black people in the South. It was his calling to affect change in the hearts of the misguided people of his city. So, almost weekly, he answered the call by traveling from north to south, planning and directing his followers in pursuit of fulfilling the goals of the Movement.

His decision to remain a "force" in the middle of Birmingham's turmoil did not come without added pain. He had initiated the challenge to all black people to fight for freedom. He had personally challenged the powerful leaders of the city and other cities throughout the south. Repeatedly, through annoying and costly legal actions, he made himself a target for the violent acts of the south's segregationists. His followers had marveled at his wit, perseverance, and bravery under fire. Many felt that the success or failure of the Movement rested heavily on the small shoulders and frame of a "little" man, who brought forth "big" ideas. A "little" man who refused to back away from hardships and disappointments. But his present situation of continuous

THE ELEVENTH COMMANDMENT:
THOU SHALT STAY OUT OF DOWNTOWN BIRMINGHAM!

DO NOT BUY BY MAIL, BY PHONE, OR IN PERSON!		FREEDOM IS NOT FREE! SACRIFICE FOR FREEDOM! STAND UP FOR FREEDOM!

DO NOT DRIFT INTO DOWNTOWN

BARGAIN BASEMENTS FOR A BOX OF TIDE AND A BAR OF IVORY SOAP!!
Do NOT Be A DRESSED UP Handkerchief-Head UNCLE TOM with No Place To Go.

SLEEPING GIANT - - - - WAKE UP!

Are you not tired of living in a city where a Negro cannot serve as a Policeman, Police-woman, or Fireman? Are you not tired of Police intimidations and brutality? Are you not tired of living in a city where Negroes SPEND $4,000,000.00 EACH week and yet NEGROES ARE NOT HIRED AS SALESMEN AND CLERKS?

Then why give a man your money and allow that man to treat you like a mangy DOG?

Get Smart—Use a dime's worth of common sense. Do not make any purchase even for 5c worth of candy from any store (large or small) in Downtown Birmingham or from any store which is a branch of a Downtown Store . . . . EVEN though the BRANCH is located in Five Points West, Roebuck Plaza, Eastwood Mall, Ensley and Bessemer.

THINK NOT OF YOURSELF, BUT OF YOUR FELLOW NEGRO BROTHERS AND THE UNBORN BOYS AND GIRLS OF THIS CITY.

MILES COLLEGE STUDENT BODY
DANIEL PAYNE COLLEGE STUDENT BODY
BOOKER T. WASHINGTON BUSINESS COLLEGE
STUDENT BODY

Flyer, "The Eleventh Commandment." (Miles College Student Body)

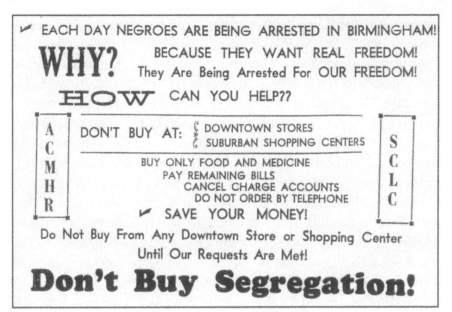

Flyer distributed by ACMHR/SCLC.

travel, and the crisis of the Movement, placed unbearable demands on him physically, emotionally, and spiritually.

During the struggles, Shuttlesworth had become instrumental in the establishment of other civil rights organizations, including the Southern Christian Leadership Conference (SCLC), which was organized in 1957. It was these ties that later allowed him to combine his forces with the forces of the Reverend Martin Luther King, Jr. and the Reverend Ralph David Abernathy. He had met Reverend Abernathy when he was a student at Alabama State College at Montgomery. He met Dr. King in the early days of 1954, when King was invited to Birmingham to speak at church service. Shuttlesworth felt that the combined forces of the ACMHR with Dr. King and the SCLC would bring the Birmingham struggle to an end. Thus, he invited to Birmingham, Dr. King and Reverend Abernathy, who up to this time had not participated in the events in Birmingham. To the dismay of segregationists, and for the benefit of the Movement, the makeup of soldiers on the battlefield of justice was about to go through a significant change. It is this change that has thus far been misreported and misunderstood by the world.

Shuttlesworth acknowledges that an age is usually named after one person, and Dr. King is that person. He understands that, "there are people in the background who do more crucial work than those in the spotlight." But Shuttlesworth was not only in the spotlight, he often was the light. Years of combat, including beatings with the brass knuckles, chains, countless arrests, and humiliating jail cells had hardened him. He had grown resistant to compromising on his principles. He strongly rejects the label imposed upon him as "rabble-rouser," stating, "people expect you to be what they want you to be, brand you with a label, and expect you to conform to their perception." By 1962, although they had become weary from continued threats, jailings and humiliations, Fred and his followers had "fought the good fight" (2 Tim. 4:7). Fred argues that the opposition failed to slow the progress of the Movement. Dr. King and the Southern Christian Leadership Conference, to this point, had been unsuccessful in challenging the very same issues in Albany, Georgia. Fred, realizing that other methods were needed, turned to Dr. King and the SCLC for support. Fred further argues, "after the failure of Albany, Dr. King and the SCLC needed Fred Shuttlesworth and the ACMHR." Regardless of their individual group needs, Fred's goal was to bring about a showdown in Birmingham through mass demonstrations, by filling the jails and dismantling segregation.

As Dr. King began his active participation in Birmingham, it was obvious that the two men were distinctly different in their approaches. But Shuttlesworth recognized the value of what King brought to the table. As Fred noted, "King was well-educated, charismatic, intelligent, and commanded the attention of his audience with his unique speaking voice and oratory skill." Shuttlesworth and King each brought a diversity that served their purpose, and their individual attributes were perfect vehicles in meeting the needs of the Movement. Without a doubt, the Lord knew what He was doing.

As the two joined together like a well-trained military force, they gathered intelligence and focused their efforts on organizing and demonstrating, which impacted almost every phase of life. The leaders recruited persons to provide taxi and transportation services, thereby negating the need to use public vehicles. Through the gathering of specific intelligence of stores and agencies that discriminated against blacks, they began to target stores and areas most vulnerable to attack. They initiated boycotts that virtually shut down stores downtown. But still, the Shuttlesworth

"The Big Three" – Shuttlesworth, Abernathy and King, Jr. during demonstrations on April 12, 1963. Courtesy of Birmingham Public Library Department of Archives and Manuscripts (Catalog number 1125.11.20A-1).

and King attack only hardened the forces of the segregationists, and made them more willing to retaliate.

Herman Poe recalls Fred's relentless efforts in leading his follow-ers in the boycotting of the major downtown businesses, including Woolworth's and Newberry's. The Movement continued to burn in the hearts of young college students from Miles College, Daniel Payne College, and Booker T. Washington Business College, who authored a flyer urging black citizens to "use a dime's worth of common sense. Do not make any purchase even for five cents worth of candy from any store." There were constant reminders that blacks spent "$4,000,000 each week," and the loss of money could be detrimental to the economic well-being of the city. As the effectiveness of the boycotts was felt, pres-sure mounted, and opposition to the Movement grew.

Following the 1956 Christmas night bombing of the Shuttlesworth par-sonage, teams of volunteers were formed to serve as "watchmen" in an effort to protect the parsonage and church from future bombings. The volunteers came from all over Birmingham, and later constructed a small shelter house across the street from the church to protect them from the elements. However, in 1958, a watchman observed a white male place a five-gallon bucket on the 33rd Street side of Bethel Baptist Church. As the bucket began to smoke, the watchman ran and grabbed the bucket, and set it approximately 50-feet across 33rd Street. Shortly thereafter, there was an explosion that shook the area. The blast blew out windows and cracked the walls of the church, but the heroics of the watchman saved the church from possible total destruction.

On Friday night, December 14, 1962, once again, dynamite was placed in the front of Bethel Baptist Church. The explosion ripped a hole in the church from the front to the rear, recalls Merrit Stoves, who remains a member of Bethel. There was extensive damage to other neighborhood homes, including the parsonage, loss of electricity, telephone service, and injuries that sent several children to the hospital. *The Birmingham News* was quick to point out that Bethel Baptist Church was a place of refuge for the "Freedom Riders," who were beaten and bombed during May 1961. Stoves is quick to praise Shuttlesworth, and remembers him for his drive. "He put himself in a lot of danger," he said.

By 1963, the trio of Shuttlesworth, King, and Abernathy were forging ahead with plans of massive civil rights demonstrations. Shuttlesworth, through his wisdom and vision, realized early how the media could play a significant role in showing the nation and the world the evil that existed in the South. He knew that using television to display this evil would help educate all the world and bring about successful change. Clearly, with the involvement of the national media, the world witnessed repeated attacks of white violence against protesters. These actual pictures would later prove to be crucial in creating national sympathy and much needed steam for the dark cloud that often hung over the Movement and demonstrators.

The dark cloud grew darker on January 14, 1963. On that day in Montgomery, Alabama, George Wallace was sworn in as governor and gave a flaming "segregation forever" speech as thousands cheered him on. That same night in Birmingham, at the Greater Seventeenth Street Apostolic Overcoming Holiness (A.O.H.) Church of God, Reverend Edward Gardner announced that the city would be a non-violent battleground. He and Shuttlesworth cautioned that George Wallace espoused a cause that was doomed.

The following weeks of meetings and plans by black leaders brought increased tension and distrust in the Birmingham community. At one point, Bull Connor dispatched detectives to the church meetings to monitor any discussion. However, the conditions and intensity of the times only resulted in growing crowds and additional bitterness. On the night of February 4, detectives W. E. Chilcoat and C. C. Ray reported the words of Gardner and Shuttlesworth: "We have got to mix politics with religion. The church must take the lead. The church has a bloody history. Shuttlesworth will be part of that bloody history." Michael Langford, now of Cincinnati, was not only baptized by Shuttlesworth, but he often listened to Fred preach about non-violence. He, like many other youths, had to endure the constant anguish and frustration experienced by their parents and friends. Langford often listened to Fred's pleas for calmness and non-violence. But even Fred's patience grew faint as he warned, "there comes a time when violence has to be met with violence." The words of Shuttlesworth were prophetic: "Even if we have to suffer pain and heartbreak. Even if some of us get bombed. We are going on with God."

As weekly meetings continued, so did the intensity. Although the crowds were large, the two detectives rapidly recorded the events of the night. By April 1963, the powerful words of Dr. King had swelled the crowds to the extent that the aisles were packed, and windows were opened to accommodate those standing outside. Bull Connor complained to the fire marshal, who declared that a fire hazard existed due to the large number of people in attendance. Shuttlesworth had the unpleasant task of directing everyone who did not have a seat to wait outside.

During this time, Birmingham was also facing a mayoral election between Connor and Albert Boutwill, a soft-spoken man who seemed more receptive to negotiating social change. Although Boutwill won the election, plans for demonstrations and picketing continued as scheduled. In the weeks that followed, Shuttlesworth, King, and Abernathy, wearing their overalls, led marchers through the streets of Birmingham. One day, Connor stood on the sidewalk as the trio and supporters marched through the streets. As Fred passed, Connor yelled, "Hey Shuttlesworth, if they see you in those clothes, they'll put you to work in the jail." Shuttlesworth, who is never lost for words, responded, "Hey, Bull, I'm trying to save the taxpayers some money."

CHAPTER 9
THE VOICES OF CHILDREN: AS THE WORLD WATCHES

On Wednesday, April 3, 1963, Reverend Shuttlesworth and Dr. King prepared their forces for additional demonstrations. They were mindful of the needed safety of their followers, and they wanted to continue their search for peaceful resolutions to the problems. Thus, they turned to two of their most dependable disciples, Lola Hendricks and Reverend Ambus Hill, Pastor of the Lily Grove Baptist Church, to apply for a Demonstration Permit at City Hall. They also realized that Bull Connor would be waiting at City Hall and could oppose their request. So, they were instructed not to challenge Connor, but to thank him and leave the facility. Lola tells the story, "When we arrived at City Hall, we were met by Bull Connor. When we asked him for the Permit, he said, 'I will picket you over to the city jail.' I thanked him and we left."

But Shuttlesworth was not to be denied. As Taylor Branch reported in *Parting The Waters*, "Shuttlesworth himself distributed copies of his *Birmingham Manifesto* to reporters. 'The patience of an oppressed people cannot endure forever... The absence of justice and progress in Birmingham demands that we make a moral witness to give our community a chance to survive."

Once again, as Shuttlesworth and King vowed to move forward, the segregationists only strengthened their opposition. As Movement organizers attempted to be served at lunch counters through sit-ins, segregationists countered by closing lunch counters. As the strategy switched to marching to City Hall, court injunctions were issued prohibiting all demonstrations. Determined to prevent integration at all costs, the city even shut off all water to public facilities, including "white" and "colored" water fountains.

It was apparent that Bull Connor was disrupting the Movement's ability to complete its mission. Connor had been successful in discouraging active participation by jailing anyone for violating onerous city laws and ordinances. Tension continued to grow within the ranks, and members were growing tired, frustrated, and disorganized. As Branch reports, "Birmingham's white leadership grew more confident that its united non-inflammatory toughness was subduing the Negro protest." However, organizers began to focus on a strategy used at the climax of James Lawson's sit-in at Nashville, Tennessee, whereby 4,000 students had marched on City Hall. Clearly, the road to a confrontation was inevitable.

A major problem faced Shuttlesworth, King and the organizers. In Birmingham, there was a court injunction against demonstrations. And because of Connor's record of arresting everyone, there was an apparent problem in getting volunteers. However, the repeated showing of the film of the Nashville demonstrations had aroused the interest of young people. Therefore, organizers set their sights on using students to participate in the marches. The leaders were toiling with the hard fact that Connor would surely arrest any child involved in the demonstrations. And further, anyone who urged children to make the march would be subject to arrest for contributing to the delinquency of a minor. This was a difficult and controversial issue for Shuttlesworth, King and other leaders. Fred insisted in the use of children, citing that "they should learn early to struggle for freedom and full citizenship." It was not an easy decision, but the leaders agreed to recruit and prepare the children for the march.

As word spread of plans to use children, young people of all ages began volunteering. They and their parents were fully briefed that their participation would almost certainly result in their arrest and jail. But those words did little to change their minds. Merrit Stoves has a vivid image of many young children, who refused to be denied this opportunity in taking an active part in effecting meaningful change on their city and their lives. "Carver High School was enclosed with a fence, and the administrators had locked the gate to keep the children inside. But they refused to stay inside, and many jumped over the fence so they could march," Stoves says.

This critical event began on Thursday, May 2, as some 1,000 children gathered in the Sixteenth Street Baptist Church. Bull Connor, having received intelligence from the FBI of the intended use of students, reinforced their daily roadblocks along the known demonstration routes. As the demonstrations began, children began making their exit from the church, singing and marching hand in hand toward downtown. Police radios repeatedly asked for paddy wagons and assistance as group after group spilled out of the church. At one point, one policeman, amazed at the reinforcement of young people, yelled at Shuttlesworth, "Hey, Fred, how many more do you have?" Shuttlesworth replied, "At least a thousand." That day, more than 600 students were taken to jail. They proudly risked their lives, always remained faithful, and believed as Sam Cooke, who later echoed their thoughts, "It's been a long time coming, but a change is gonna come."

On Friday, May 3, once again, some 1,000 students convened in Sixteenth Street Baptist Church and prepared for another date in history. However, Bull Connor and the segregationists once again had a defensive strategy. Across from the church, Connor had positioned a massive force of police in front of school buses. They were reinforced by police cruisers and fire equipment, mounted with high-powered hoses. The fire trucks were equipped with special "monitor guns," which the fire department had advertised as miracles of long-range fire fighting. The guns were capable of knocking bricks loose from mortar, or stripping bark from a tree at a distance of 100 feet. These powerful and deadly weapons were directed at the front of the church. As the students again made their exit from the church, they were ordered to disperse. When they continued, orders were given to spray them with water from the fire hoses.

As the first wave of water hit, the children were shocked and disoriented. Some withdrew, but others with resolve joined together and began singing "freedom" to the tune of "Amen." As the students continued their defiance, orders were given to pound them again. The firemen responded by advancing toward them and pounding them at close range, ripping clothes and skin from their bodies. Children were literally pummeled and thrown around like rag dolls.

Connor had carefully planned for the use of every type of action. Where he was lacking in manpower, he deployed Police K-9 units, which unleashed vicious attacks on children and innocent bystanders. Branch observed,

"On a street corner outside the Jockey Boy restaurant, two dog teams came up behind a group of awed spectators who did not notice them until one of the handlers seized a 15-year-old boy and whirled him around into the jaws of a German shepherd. An AP photographer standing nearby caught the sight that came to symbolize Birmingham: a white policeman in dark sunglasses grasping a Negro boy by the front of the shirt as his other hand gave just enough slack in the leash for the dog to spring upward and bury its teeth in the boy's abdomen. And most compelling was the boy himself, who was tall, thin, and well dressed, leaning into the attacking dog with an arm dropped submissively at his side and a straight-ahead look of dead calm on his face."

Birmingham's leaders, expecting a public outcry and sympathy, blamed their use of force on the lawlessness of the demonstrators. The events of the day quickly gained the attention of President Kennedy, who sent his representative, Burke Marshall, to bring calm and reach a mutual peace agreement. Shuttlesworth became suspicious of Marshall's efforts, declaring that Marshall was only helping whites maintain segregated negotiations. For the next several days, negotiations and demonstrations continued. On Tuesday, May 7, Shuttlesworth and organizers used a strategy of deploying demonstrators from a variety of locations in an effort to split the police forces and avoid immediate arrest.

Shuttlesworth himself was to lead demonstrators from the Sixteenth Street Baptist Church. He well knew that the firemen were relentless in the continued use of the dangerous and deadly fire hoses. In one instance, the hoses were inadvertently turned on a policeman and cracked his ribs. On this day, as Shuttlesworth appeared with his line of singing children, the firemen directed the monitor gun on him. The powerful impact of water lifted his body from the pavement, slammed him against the wall, pinning him to the church until he collapsed. As the ambulance took him away, Bull Connor was heard saying, "I wish they had carried him away in a hearse."

As the violence prolonged, the Kennedy administration scrambled and considered every possible solution to resolve the conflict. Dr. King had become a primary mediator and maintained an open line of communication with the Kennedy administration. As negotiations continued through the night, the administration believed it had reached a settlement agreeable to both sides. The opposition forces claimed they wanted to work toward a peaceful resolution, but argued that it was difficult to negotiate as long as the demonstrations continued. On Wednesday morning, May 8, King, after completing a round-the-clock meeting with Marshall and white negotiators, spread word of a proposed one-day moratorium on demonstrations. However, there was one significant piece missing from the puzzle. King and others failed to take into consideration that Shuttlesworth, due to his injury on the previous day, was in the hospital and did not participate, nor was he consulted regarding the proposed agreements.

King, Marshall and others had convened at the home of John Drew.

Andrew Young was sent to the hospital to see if Shuttlesworth was able to come to the Drew home for a final meeting on the moratorium. Learning of the meeting, Shuttlesworth became frantic, checked himself out of the hospital, and had his wife and Reverend Gardner drive him to the Drew home. Still sedated from medication, he was furious with King and anyone who considered any agreement without consulting with him. Fred had a long and proud history of fighting for civil rights in Birmingham. Just the previous day he suffered from the deadly blast of the monitor gun. He had suffered from beatings, bombings, and constant mental and physical abuse.

Birmingham was his undertaking. It was he who had given birth to the Movement. And although God was responsible for its growth, he had provided the food and drink. It was he who cradled and rocked its followers when they became weary. It was he who often had diagnosed the various causes of illness and prescribed the appropriate medication. And it was he, the General, who had led his forces through fierce battles and never lost his faith and courage. Further, although King was busy in negotiations, Shuttlesworth was still deeply disturbed that King had not come to visit him in the hospital.

Now, Shuttlesworth was hearing "King's" plans for a truce. Branch summarizes the fiery explosion of Shuttlesworth as he entered the Drew home:

Replicas of the deadly "monitor guns." (Photo courtesy of Lucious Washington and Lola Hendricks)

Replica of German shepherd dogs. (Photo courtesy of Lucious Washington and Lola Hendricks)

"Say that again. Did I hear you right? Well, Martin, who decided? You're in a hell of a fix, young man." As King tried vainly to calm him, an aide pointed out that the matter was 'moot because King already had scheduled a press conference.' This only inflamed Shuttlesworth's sarcasm, "Oh, you've got a press conference?" he asked in mock wonder. "I thought we were going to make a joint statement." Daring King to announce a truce, he promised to nullify it by leading the kids right back into the streets.

Others were stunned. Marshall had been assuring Washington (the White House) that the matter was being resolved, but now Shuttlesworth, as the media anxiously awaited, was threatening to bring embarrassment to him and the administration. Marshall attempted to impress upon Shuttlesworth the importance of this event.

"There have been promises made," he said. Branch wrote,

"What promises?" shouted Shuttlesworth. The reference to unknown understandings backfired, as did Abernathy's soothing suggestion that perhaps Shuttlesworth was sick after all and should go back to the hospital. He was leaving all right, Shuttlesworth stormed, but they had better understand that neither King nor President Kennedy himself could call off the afternoon march. "Wait a minute, Fred," King said softly. Over his shoulder to Marshall, he stressed the obvious vulnerabilities facing leaders of a small national minority. "We've got to have unity, Burke," he said, "We've got to have unity." Shuttlesworth bridled at hearing the call imposed for once upon him. "I'll be dammed if you'll have it like this!" he roared at King. "You're Mister Big, but you're going to be Mister S-H-I-T!"

Shuttlesworth still has a vivid image of that day. "As I entered the Drew home, Dr. King was standing, looking out the window with his hands in his back pockets." Fred continues, "At first, he didn't say anything, and I said, 'Martin, why must I get out of my sick bed and come up here?' Martin did not reply." Imagine the tension as Fred stood there staring at Dr. King. Fred repeated, "Martin, why did I have to come up here?" Martin then replied, "Fred, we got to call the demonstrations off." "I said, 'What?' But then suddenly there was a response from Deanie Drew, John's wife, who asked, 'I want to know why we can't call it off!'" Deanie, because of her light skin, could easily pass as being white by anyone who did not know her. When King and the SCLC came to Birmingham, she was used to penetrate some of the stores where Negroes couldn't go. She often provided transportation to Dr. King, who usually used their home for living and meeting quarters.

However, her comments to Fred were untimely and disturbing. Fred shouted back, "Deanie, I didn't come here to talk to you. You didn't call anything on, and you can't call anything off." He directed his attention back to Dr. King. "Now Martin, why in the hell do you want to call it off?" Fred realized that Dr. King was being pressured by the government and the special interests of the middle class to resolve the problems and stop the demonstrations. He contends that there was a conspiracy by the opposition to undermine everything he had done by convincing Dr. King to denounce the Movement and leave Birmingham.

Apparently, Shuttleworth was quite accurate. On July 25, 1998, Ambassador Andrew Young, while speaking at the Southern Christian Leadership Conference President's Inauguration, spoke about those times and relived some of the painful memories. He recalled how thousands of young people had surrendered their freedom and accepted the painful consequences of being housed in the many jails arranged by Bull Connor. Segregationists used these and other circumstances in applying pressure on Dr. King to leave the city. Ambassador Young stated, "There was a lot of people advising him to leave town and say Fred Shuttleworth was wrong, and that we couldn't break the back of Birmingham."

Fred continues, "Burke Marshall sat across from me, staring, as if I was Jesus Himself. He spoke only twice. The first time he said, 'I've made promises to these people.' But I responded that any promises he may have made in Birmingham without my approval were not promises. The second time he spoke was when I got up from my chair and, with the help of Reverend Gardner and my wife, staggered to my feet. Burke looked me straight in the eye and said, 'Don't worry, Fred, they'll agree to your demands.'"

Fred's demands consisted of four points:
1) Desegregation of lunch counters, rest rooms and drinking fountains, to be completed over a period of 90-days;
2) Better job opportunities;
3) Bond relief on all jailed demonstrators; and
4) Further communications from white negotiators.

Shuttlesworth was insulted with what appeared to be the basis for the one day moratorium. He let it be known that King was giving in to demands at a time when the demonstrations were at their climax and the Movement was capable of achieving everything it wanted. White leaders had argued that they could not continue to negotiate while the demonstrations were ongoing. Therefore, King, as a gesture of "good faith" consented to call off the marches. But Shuttlesworth countered, "Martin, you didn't call a damn thing on, and you ain't going to call a damn thing off."

In the view of Shuttlesworth, there was no reason to give in at this time. He warned King that if he announced any agreement without his consent, he would direct his followers to again take to the streets, which had the probability of setting off more violent confrontations.

During the heated discussion, "the telephone rang, it was Robert Kennedy," Shuttlesworth recalls. Marshall's assistant was called to the telephone and was heard making reference to Shuttlesworth as the "frail one" and as being a slight problem. "I shouted, 'Tell Bob, yes I'm frail, but not that damn frail; and nobody is going to call the demonstrations off,'" Fred says. As he continued his conversation with Kennedy, intense tension could be felt in the room. Shuttlesworth, still in pain from the fire hose attack, stood his ground. The national spotlight was focused intently on Birmingham now. The decisions rendered here would have serious political consequences. This was of little concern to Shuttlesworth, who had endured more than his share of racial evil.

Since 1940, he had fought and endured the abuse of segregation. He had seen segregationists use Negro against Negro to "maintain the system." He reflects, "Everybody, including King, thought I would be the first to be killed." And now, at a moment when the first major decision was to be made, he was not consulted. He had demands which must be met, and he was not about to settle for anything less. Marshall, finally realizing that Shuttlesworth was not frail, sought to satisfy Shuttlesworth and bring about a peaceful end to this southern explosion. The demands were major obstacles to those in opposition to the Movement. Marshall had little choice. He assured Shuttlesworth that he would get his demands, and on May 10, 1963, Shuttlesworth was the lead speaker at a news conference announcing the terms of the settlement.

Shuttlesworth had been responsible for lighting a fire in Birmingham that ignited fury in black people all over the south. It had given them the encouragement to challenge racism for what it was. "If Jesus meant anything, then segregation was wrong," he says. At the press conference, reporters from all over the country were present. However, they did not know Shuttlesworth or the long and vigorous training he provided to his followers in Birmingham. King had become well known, and was well-respected by the White House. Thus, the reporters sought to hear the terms of the settlement from him. As King spoke, Shuttlesworth, still recovering from his fire hose attack and exhaustion, collapsed, and was again taken to the hospital. Branch relates how Fred, appearing several days later, spoke in his old vigor, "I have just about de-bulled ol' Bull Conner! I didn't know it would take me seven years."

The arrests and violent attacks against the children proved to be the ultimate downfall of Connor. There were more than 3,000 demonstrators jailed, which created a congested jail and court system throughout Birmingham and surrounding counties. Herman Poe often watched and felt helpless, seeing children being treated like cattle as they were herded into a fenced area around the jail on 6th Street South. Since the jail had over-flowed, the fence served to house and contain the demonstrators.

Audrey Faye Hendricks was nine years old. But she too refused to sit on the side lines. Even at that tender age, she felt the necessity of her presence. With the blessings of her parents, little Audrey marched. And as expected, she too was arrested. "The worst thing I thought was that they might kill me...I was in jail seven days. We slept in little rooms with bunk beds. There were about 12 of us in a room. I was in a room with my friends. We called ourselves Freedom Fight-ers, Freedom Riders," she said.

The combined forces of Shuttlesworth, King, the SCLC, and the ACMHR had predicted that Bull Connor, in his last days as Police Commissioner, might respond violently to demonstrations against seg-regation. A major demonstration dramatizing this evil to the entire nation, they believed, might result in federal legislation outlawing seg-regation. The manner in which Connor responded gained national and world attention and brought instant scorn on Birmingham. So, this team approach proved accurate, for the Birmingham demonstra-tions were the major motivation for the Kennedy Administration's in-troduction of the legislation that became the Civil Rights Act of 1964.

During the Civil Rights Movement, meetings were routinely held at the Sixteenth Street Baptist Church, a key landmark in America's civil rights history. Shuttlesworth and King had used this holy place as a forum to successfully stir emotions of blacks. And although their relentless voices instilled fear in many whites, their goal was to bring about meaningful racial and social change. This historic monument was the cornerstone for the final stages of the Movement. It was the place where nightly Mass Meetings were held, exhorting citizens to act, and it was the place where strategies were planned.

As the trumpets sounded to end the street demonstrations, and both sides focused on the agenda of reconciliation, this church represented a true symbol for peace and progress. Throughout the city of Birmingham, violence and bombings had become common modes of attack against demonstrators and organizers. Since the 1940s, there had been repeated bombings which were common occurrences. Following the Shuttlesworth and King peace agreement, sporadic bombings continued as a reminder that the battle against racial hatred was far from complete.

However, organizers and Birmingham's committed leaders may have failed to realize how much deadly venom remained within this wounded animal of hatred. That is, until Sunday morning, September

Shuttlesworth and Dr. King during an appearance in Cincinnati following the ending of demonstrations in Birmingham. (Submitted by Reverend Shuttlesworth.)

15, 1963, when worshippers gathered in the Sixteenth Street Baptist Church for Sunday services. Four months had passed since the peace agreement, but segragationists had a final message to deliver. It was a Sunday, like so many that preceded it. A Sunday that witnessed the doors of the church opening, allowing to enter four young girls: Denise McNair, age 11; Cynthia Wesley, age 14; Addie Mae Collins, age 14; and Carol Robertson, age 16. But, unlike any other Sunday, this day saw the devastating aftermath of 16 sticks of dynamite placed at the basement door by the Ku Klux Klan. The blast resulted in the deaths of the four girls, who were changing into their choir robes after attending Sunday School classes in the basement.

This murderous act re-ignited tension and anger, but now blacks were on the verge of fighting back with all out violence. Shuttlesworth and King hurried to Birmingham to urge an embattled people to remain calm and maintain a non-violent approach. A Mass Meeting was held to bring order and direction to an angry and frightened community. Even demonstrations were discouraged. Shuttlesworth, in explaining the decision, stated, "I want this to be a period of mourning, not demonstrations and protest. I think we can best show the world the horror of this crime by our solemn mourning."

This horrendous act lay heavily on the conscience of Birmingham for all the world to see. It was not merely an act against man, it was an attack against God's creation. It penetrated the hearts and souls of even the young. Recalling the horrible week of terror and tension in Birmingham following the dynamite bombing, the mother of one of the little victims told how her son came running to her from the wrecked temple with blood streaming down his face. He quietly asked, "Mama, where was God?"

Historic Sixteenth Street Baptist Church. (Photo courtesy of Lucious Washington and Lola Hendricks.)

But Fred Shuttlesworth felt God's presence years earlier. That presence directed him to take action and help others realize His presence. Still, people tend to see Fred Shuttlesworth in the shadow of Dr. King. Fred is often asked about the contributions of King, while little and sometimes no attention is given to him. However, it is apparent that he deserves credit for being a primary leader of civil rights throughout the country. As Fred reflects,

"I wanted to defeat segregation, and I was not concerned about any other distractions. I think without my presence and without what I did, King could not have done what he did. I never was hung up on getting (emotional pause)... but King would not have received the Nobel Peace Prize if it had not been for Birmingham. Martin did not ask me to go to Norway with him. He carried a lot of people (emotional pause)... but that's, that's men, we are all men, not angels. King would not have a holiday if it had not been for Birmingham. We would not have won the struggle if it had not been for Fred Shuttlesworth. I think he slighted me in some way, but I never took personally what King did or failed to do. But if God strikes me down tomorrow, you need to know that King was a 'voice.' He was a 'prophetic voice' who was capable of articulating. He was able to reach men's hearts."

King did reach many hearts. And yes, Fred did play a significant role in defeating segregation, at least the visible signs of its poison. However, after hundreds of years of social and racial injustice, Fred is still concerned that the cancer remains. His fight with Bull Connor and Birmingham's problems was just scraping the surface of much deeper issues.

Theophilus Eugene Connor, born July 11, 1897 in Selma, Alabama, was relentless in his efforts to maintain segregation at all costs. He espoused a clear message that mixing the races would damage the nation. Connor's racist philosophy continued in Alabama following the May 10, 1963 agreement. Connor continued to push his racist agenda as President of the Alabama Public Service Commission (PSC). And even after suffering a stroke in December 1966 that confined him to a wheelchair, he clung to his "doomed" beliefs. A second stroke, in late February 1973 and almost two weeks of suffering, brought his life to an end in early March 1973.

CHAPTER 10
THE BIRMINGHAM CIVIL RIGHTS INSTITUTE

The dreams of the black community were in concert with the dreams of every white American – to live together in peace; to enjoy the freedoms of speech and religion; to find equality, liberty and justice for all; to offer their children a safe and promising tomorrow; and to seek a better life. Not only were Southern blacks failing to accomplish their dreams, they were often dared to dream. As a young boy, Shuttlesworth had dreamed, and continued to dream. And as he rallied his followers, his prophetic words and deeds have become forever etched in civil rights history. In 1953, he returned to Birmingham prepared to lead the charge for those who were willing to endure pain and heartbreak. He would encourage and motivate those who lost their jobs. He espoused the good from the worst bombings. And daily, he kept the faith and chose to follow God.

Upon his return, Shuttlesworth challenged the Birmingham establishment and set the tone for future leaders. What happened in Birmingham reached far beyond the borders of that city. The experiences of its trials affected an entire nation. Shuttlesworth and Birmingham led the march to abolish the barriers, brutality and the institutional ugliness that Southern blacks endured in everyday life. The entire ordeal had a valuable history…a history that needed to be harnessed, protected and shared for future generations. There were well-established colleges and universities which were organized and offered less in the form of total education to the academic arena. Truly, the civil rights movement was deserving of its own institution to educate, inform and display, not for bitterness, but for understanding and healing.

The Reverend Fred L. Shuttlesworth and the Movement were deserving of a shrine to forever honor their contributions to all of society. Thus, let it be known to all that:

- Thirty-nine years after Shuttlesworth made his return to Birmingham, accepted the pastorate at Bethel Baptist Church, and began challenging segregationists;
- Thirty-six years after the NAACP was outlawed in Birmingham and throughout the south, and Shuttlesworth founded the Alabama Christian Movement for Human Rights (ACMHR);
- Thirty-six years after 101 southern senators and representatives in the U.S. Congress published the "Southern Manifesto," calling on states to disobey and resist school desegregation;
- Thirty-six years after the Ku Klux Klan bombed the home of Shuttlesworth and his family;
- Twenty-nine years after the police dog and firehose attack in Birmingham on innocent children;
- Twenty-nine years after the Ku Klux Klan bombed the Sixteenth Street Baptist Church, killing four black adolescent girls;
- Twenty-four years after the assassination of the Reverend Martin Luther King, Jr.;
- Thirteen years after a task force was formed to consider establishing an institute to protect the treasures of the Movement;
- Seven years after the land was bought;
- And, two years after the City of Birmingham sold the Social Security Administration's Southeastern Program Service Center to fund construction after two defeated bond proposals, the Birmingham Civil Rights Institute officially opened its doors on November 15, 1992, as a living monument to the struggle for equality.

Organizers and the City of Birmingham rightfully paid honor and tribute to Reverend Fred L. Shuttlesworth by erecting a bronze statue of his likeness in front of the Institute. Created both as a museum and an Institute, Birmingham is willing to expose its past and use it as a guidepost for the future. Mayor Richard Arrington, in an open letter to the Citizens of Birmingham, echoed its major premise,

"The Institute is a number of things. It is a forum that fosters learning, a museum, a tribute, thought-provoking archives, and a monument to a struggle that left us all better for it." Arrington further recognized that the Institute "presents the essence of equal opportunity and justice for all citizens, resulting in a brighter future for us and for our children. It is indeed a Place of Revolution that has given way to Reconciliation. The Institute offers endless educational opportunities with events, expediencies and exhibits that appeal to everyone."

It is more than an account of what happened during the Civil Rights Era in Birmingham and in the South. The galleries, divided into three primary sections, create an experience of the Civil Rights Movement. The first section, called Barriers, is designed to give a realistic view of what everyday life was like for blacks in Birmingham. Exhibits include: white and colored drinking fountains; an iron ore mine symbolizing a major employer of blacks who were relegated to manual-labor jobs; a church, the center of the black community; two schools, one white and one black, showing that separate but equal usually meant separate and unequal as limited resources went first to the white community and then to the black; a courtroom, where black defendants were placed on trial before white judges, juries and prosecutors.

The second section, Confrontation, presents to the visitors a gallery of art that introduces various attitudes about race.

And the final section, a series of galleries called *Movement* is designed to help the visitor better understand the troubled times of the Civil Rights Movement. Major exhibits include:

- Films on the Freedom Riders, Dr. King's "I Have A Dream" speech on the steps of the Lincoln Memorial, and the dog and fire-hose attacks on demonstrators;
- A statue of Rosa Parks, who refused to give up her bus seat in Montgomery, Alabama;
- A jail cell, the actual bars and a replica of the Birmingham jail cell where King was kept and where he wrote, "Letter from the Birmingham Jail."

Throughout the museum, visitors are bombarded by waves of sound, hundreds of still images, galleries of moving pictures and historical artifacts. There are plenty of vivid reminders of the long struggle to desegregate interstate busing, as blacks and whites rode together as Freedom Riders. Included is a brief summary of activities in Albany, Georgia; Greenwood, Mississippi; and Rock Hill, South Carolina, as blacks continued the fight for the right to vote, gain meaningful employment, and eat in public dining facilities.

When founders of the Birmingham Civil Rights Institute were in their planning stages, they turned to Lola Hendricks, who had amassed valuable documents and artifacts while serving as Correspondence Secretary to Shuttlesworth and to the ACMHR. She immediately began going through her files to find documents and relics of the Movement. And any documents she could not find, she contacted friends who assisted her in locating needed artifacts. Many of the documents contained in the Institute's archives came from her search and her records. She takes great pride in her work and love for history by saving everything, especially newspapers and articles.

Scholars from around the world marvel at the painful, but rich history bestowed behind the walls of the Institute. It provides an opportunity to gain knowledge about the struggle for black equality that took place in the "Deep South." It is one of Birmingham's institutions where everyone can be educated and learn about race issues and civil rights. Take the burned bus, a replica of the buses that transported the Freedom Riders. Its massive structure and placement at the Freedom Riders display often surprises some viewers, while reliving painful memories for others.

The history reflected in this display is that of the bloody Washington, DC to New Orleans bus ride that began in early May 1961 by seven blacks and six whites. Their goal was to confront the system of segregation on interstate buses in the South. The display reminds its visitors of the ugly scene faced by the riders just outside the city of Anniston, Alabama, where a bus was stopped by a white mob and suffered the devastation of a fire bomb which was thrown inside. As riders fled, they were beaten by the mob. Visitors also face the scene of the second bus, which arrived later in Birmingham, only to face a larger mob. They, too, were severely beaten, just two blocks from the police station.

The voice of Mrs. Hendricks speaks for many: "I get a chill when I see that bus. It still looks real. I can remember when two white men, who were members of the Freedom Riders, came to our house for

Statues depicting jailed children during the 1963 demonstrations. (Photo courtesy of Lucious Washington and Lola Hendricks.)

refuge. They were all smoked and dirty, and we took them in for the night." She adds, "Visitors are often mesmerized by exhibits such as the schoolroom or the water fountain, which depicts the vast differences between blacks and whites, and the injustice of segregation. But the bus often remains a focal point of attraction."

She is now working as a volunteer at the Birmingham Civil Rights Institute and serves as a member of the Oral History Advisory Committee at the Institute. She has received numerous awards for her involvement in the Church and Civil Rights activities. She was awarded, "The Legacy of the Dreamer Award," presented to her on December 9, 1994, at the Alabama Southern Christian Leadership Conference convention in Anniston, Alabama. And, on September 6, 1995, she was recognized by the National Baptist Convention, Inc., with the Award for Faithful and Continuous Contributions to the cause of Freedom and Justice for all People. And on November 1, 1998, she stood proud as a co-author of the book, *Walk To Freedom,* which provides its readers with significant photographs, news articles, accounts of Reverend Shuttlesworth, Birmingham churches, organizers, and followers of this difficult era in American history.

The massive, state-of-the-art facility is located at the corner of historic 16th Street and 6th Avenue North. It is truly a shrine, and it should not serve to aggravate deep-seeded wounds of the old-South. Odessa Woolfolk, President, remarks, "Through the establishment of the Birmingham Civil Rights Institute, we are saying we no longer hide from our history." She continues, "We recognize that we were once a city that housed two people, black and white, unknown to one another except through the long painful thread of segregation. Now we are a different city, embracing our past and through the Civil Rights Institute, we are utilizing it as a guidepost for the future."

As the statue of Rev. Fred L. Shuttlesworth greets every visitor, the Institute, among other things, is a continued symbol of his courage, his strength, and his determination to bring equality to all mankind.

Statue of Reverend Fred L. Shuttlesworth in front of the Birmingham Civil Rights Institute. (Photo courtesy of Lucious Washington and Lola Hendricks.)

CHAPTER 11
A NEW BEGINNING

Following the explosive ending of 1963, Shuttlesworth devoted more time to his congregation in Cincinnati. He does not wish to upstage Dr. King or de-emphasize the significance of King's involvement in Birmingham. As he speaks of King with much respect, he fully accepts the fact that King was blessed with different talents and skills. He quickly acknowledges that there were differences between them. He regrets their most famous disagreement involving King's decision to call a one-day moratorium on demonstrations. However, he explains that he felt betrayed. Shuttlesworth and King had joined forces in an effort to fight for freedom. They had agreed that there would be a daily meeting to discuss and plan their strategy. However, he felt left out of some of the most significant discussions that determined the outcome of all his efforts. King's proposed truce and moratorium not only failed to include him, but it did not include some major issues that Shuttlesworth was committed to attaining.

Some who worked with Shuttlesworth labeled him as difficult and domineering. Fred simply replies, "I had a job to do. If people thought I was difficult, they all have their opinions."

Others, like Herman Poe, consider Shuttlesworth a "great man." He adds, "There are so many wonderful things he did for this city. And I don't think anybody else would have stood up to Bull Connor." Michael Langford admired the energy and commitment of his former pastor. Langford is proud of being baptized by Shuttlesworth, and adds, "Many claim to be a legend in their own mind, but 'the Reverend' is a legend in his own time."

Ruby Fredricka, named after her mother and father, now laughs about the strong discipline that was administered by her father. But the man lived a life that demanded discipline. Fred, Jr. chuckles, saying, "We would often call him 'Zoro,' because he would pull his belt out and make a 'Z' like the T.V. character." Their mother, Ruby, died in February 1971 after falling down some stairs. Their divorce earlier may have been another casualty of the Movement. The subject of their mother is very difficult for Fred, Jr. and Ruby. The pain and agony can easily be detected in their voices and movements. "It is just too personal for us. She is not here today because of this. Everything about what happened is just unpleasant. Black and white people were disrespectful to her," Fred says.

Shuttlesworth's magic and fame were not so well accepted in Cincinnati. In 1965, Revelation Baptist Church members virtually split in half amid accusations that Shuttlesworth was "too dictatorial" and "mishandled church funds." As a result, about 200 of Revelation's 800 members left with Shuttlesworth and formed the Greater New Light Baptist Church. In 1977, the membership, under the leadership of Shuttlesworth, built its current facility, located in North Avondale of Cincinnati.

On Monday, June 2, 1969, Reverend Shuttlesworth addressed the 13th Annual Conference of the ACMHR at Birmingham, Alabama, and delivered the following message:

> Mr. Vice President, Officers, and Members of the Alabama Christian Movement for Human Rights.
>
> We meet tonight on our thirteenth Annual Occasion as a Civil Rights Organization still committed to the causes of equal justice, brotherhood, and peace – those elusive qualities without which the American dream will never be fulfilled. We meet in our continuing commitment to the fulfillment of that dream, though our unsettled times and national mood cast a lingering shadow over the prospects that the Civil Rights Organizations of this country can soon accomplish their goal.
>
> Indeed, it must be admitted that the country appears more divided than ever; that continued disillusionment among people may give rise to even more discord and disunity; and

Greater New Light Baptist Church, founded by Shuttlesworth in Cincinnati. (Courtesy of PCA International, Inc.)

that our governmental structures discern very slowly the real needs of the communities, and move even more slowly, and with too little, seeking to meet these needs. The confrontations and turmoil on college campuses and over the Vietnam War have engrossed the national attention; and when combined with the overblown call for Black Separatism, these tend to blot out in people's minds the shades of difference in the protest Movements. A recent magazine editorialized that the Dreamer is dead and his dream seems impossible of fulfillment.

But the Dream cannot die because it is the foundation of this Republic, and is based upon a moral code older than the mountains; and claims as a Father from whom that Brotherhood must come, the God who founded this universe and endowed mankind with certain privileges and opportunities. Martin Luther King, Jr., is sleeping in death, but the spirit of Truth and Righteousness to which he gave himself is even more alive because of his sacrifice. The cause of Civil Liberties and the right of legitimate protest are firmly anchored and understood in our land because of the life he lived and the paths he walked.

There is indeed violence in our system: injustice in its Courts, inequities in its treatment of and care for its citizens, reliance upon military arms for its economy and international posture, unequal treatment of its minorities, etc. This latent violence has spawned a reaction now being manifested in riots, burnings, seizing buildings, confrontations with police forces, and a growing disregard of established institutions. And though violence has taken from us great men like King, John and Robert Kennedy, Medgar Evers, and many others, we see in their lives the continuing commitment to truth, non-violence, nobility of spirit and purpose; and we are persuaded that it is better to love than to hate.

But the example of the Christ of the Cross and the Resurrection guarantees that Truth must win even if violence of whatever nature, temporarily overwhelms it. His words tell us to overcome evil with good. To me this means telling men the truth about themselves, whether good or bad. That they are sons of God and brothers by creation, and that they must struggle for brotherhood and unity against all forces organized against it. That all men and every man must know dignity and the worth of the individual. That men, black and white, should organize their Communities as brothers and work together without hate and strife for the rights and privileges of all the people. That everybody is a somebody; and that no man, law or institution will be allowed to rob even "the least of these" of his dignity.

Moses was told to go out and "stir up the people that they would want to be free." This makes me know that God wants people enlightened as to who they are and who He is; and that the Social Gospel means more Community organization with enlightenment and encouragement to all; and that men who are engaged in a worthy cause with righteous motives and methods should pursue it persistently even to death. For he who loses his life for the sake of the Righteous Gospel shall find it.

So my friends, we dare not let up the struggle for justice and equality now. The non-violent Movement has permanently established the right to peaceful and legitimate protest. It has started a re-thinking of the democratic processes themselves, and a re-ordering of priorities and values in America. Laws guaranteeing human dignity are on the books, and will be implemented according to our degree of protestations.

I salute you as a valiant group of men and women who began 13 years ago really caring and daring. I salute you for your loyalty and devotion to duty, and for persevering in the face of stark danger and overcoming a multitude of obstacles placed in your path. The World now knows of your suffering and trials during the terror of KKK bombings, Bull Connor's dogs and jails, and the vicious mal-administration of justice in Alabama Courts. You have been strong, not with guns, but with courage. And combining forces in 1963-65 with Dr. King and SCLC, you started the Nation to really pray, think and commit itself to actually bringing about justice in the U.S. I commend all the Officers and Members who have worked so very closely with me for these 13 years.

The basis for continued Movement Progress is laid. The danger of State and Local Officials destroying this group is past, and a national symbol of the Movement as Leader is not necessary for its continued existence. This is why I have remained as President since October 1966, at your request. Also, there were criminal cases against me which held the fate over a thousand local people here; and my commitment would not let me leave them in danger. If any would have had to serve their sentences, the first would have had to be me. The U.S. Supreme Court in March wiped clean the slate against me, and in so doing freed 1,500 others. The last three years I have worked through the Central Committee. There is now need for wider and more community organization. I resign tonight as President of the Organization, and I recommend Rev. Gardner to the Post. But you have the right to select anyone you choose.

I shall remain President only to hold two executive meetings to set final details; and give you time to select a President if you do not follow my choice. But under no circumstances will I remain President longer than the close of the Annual SCLC Convention in August. God bless and be with you.

Shuttlesworth has continued to be an outspoken voice for freedom. He is often disappointed with the attitudes of blacks in Cincinnati. He readily asserts, "In Cincinnati, blacks are divided in ideals and understanding of what the Movement represented and accomplished." He further assesses that they have their own "agenda." However, at age 77, he remains active for the cause of human rights and freedom. He continues to reach out and lift up those who, for whatever reason, have not been able to realize the American dream.

Ruby proudly acknowledges that her father, in 1988, donated $100,000 from a previous real estate investment, and formed the Shuttlesworth Housing Foundation, which sought to help poor people buy their own homes. "He had been struck by the number of families close to the poverty line who needed no more than modest help to become homeowners," wrote *The Cincinnati Enquirer*.

Jim Flessa of Cincinnati's Better Housing League, summarizes: "Shuttlesworth advertised in the local newspaper that he was willing to provide the funds to help the needy in the purchase of a home. The Better Housing League, committed to helping people in the purchase and retention of a home, and concerned that a process would be required to help those most in need, offered its assistance in screening and counseling applicants." Flessa adds that the Foundation was incorporated in June 1988, received its tax exemption status in September 1988, and made its first grant in January 1989.

On March 15, 1991, the Foundation became a managed fund to the Greater Cincinnati Foundation. Also, in March 1991, the Foundation received its first major contribution, a $5,000 grant from Central Trust Bank of Cincinnati. A short time later, in June 1991, Fifth Third Bank, trustees for the Jacob G. Schmidlapp Trust, stepped forward with a $50,000 grant. Private donations have exceeded $150,000, thanks to Fred's concern and desire to lift up the needy so that they too may fulfill their dream. And beginning in 1997, the City of Cincinnati began supplementing the Foundation with a contribution of $130,000 annually. By December 1998, the Foundation had proudly assisted and funded more than 380 families in the purchase of a home.

And although the man who "dared" to dream, and challenge the likes of Bull Connor; who refused, as it was often expected, to bow his head when talking to whites, but demanded to be treated as an equal; who withstood the pain and punishment of numerous beatings, bombings of his home and church, and continued to suffer persecutions in the court system, to this day, is usually viewed "only" as the assistant of Dr. King. But his image has risen among whites who have come to appreciate his heroism to a worthy cause. In addition to his statue greeting all who visit the Birmingham Civil Rights Institute, Birmingham, in 1988, renamed a street in his honor. And in November 1998, the City of Cincinnati, in further recognizing this man's many contributions, renamed North and South Crescent Streets to Shuttlesworth Circle (North and South).

Some three decades after his violent confrontations in Birmingham, Shuttlesworth still takes pride in recognizing Birmingham as his home. He harbors no bitterness for the many segregationists and racists who inflicted great harm on him and others. He merely wanted what every American wanted and what the Constitution guarantees. This legendary pioneer, in his own right, maintains a very active schedule accepting requests to speak at events, conferences, colleges and universities throughout the country. Several years ago, he was even invited to the White House.

Shuttlesworth and President Clinton in May, 1996.

Former Ohio Secretary of State Bob Taft (now Governor of Ohio) presented the Robert A. Taft Award for life-long housing achievement to Reverend Fred L. Shuttlesworth, May 1996. (Courtesy of Better Housing League of Greater Cincinnati.)

In August 1995, The National Action Network, a nationwide civil rights group based in Washington, D.C., requested his support in protest against U.S. Supreme Court Justice Clarence Thomas, who they claimed to be "anti-civil rights." Thomas, the only African-American on the bench, had been voting against civil rights issues since his appointment in 1991 by President George Bush. Thomas, in the case *Adarand Constructors vs. Pena*, wrote "...Government cannot make us equal; it can only recognize, respect and protect us as equal before the law...." Shuttlesworth argues, "He advanced to his position because of affirmative action. His own story of coming from a lowly status, and advancing to this level, should make him a strong proponent of affirmative action. For him to suggest that the playing field is now level and everything is all right is totally unwise."

Reverend Fred Shuttlesworth is quite familiar with playing fields. As a gifted warrior who experienced nearly every facet of suffering, he stands ready to defend the rights of the indigent and abused. He submits, "My life has been dedicated to lifting people. It's been a glorious struggle." Very few people realize his many struggles. How this man disciplined himself by completing all academic requirements in obtaining, in 1950, a BS Degree from Alabama State College; in 1951, a BS Degree from Selma University; and subsequent completion of 16-credit hours in Master of Science degree studies at Alabama State College. However, his struggles are further acknowledged as a recepient of Honorary Degrees from various colleges and universities.

Historians may never accurately write a book to tell his story, but little does it matter to him. His glory appears to be in the good news of another story. It is a story unmatched, which he acknowledges as he clutches his Bible and proudly says, "Nobody can ever write a book as good as this one."

The Bible is a vivid symbol of Fred's sense of freedom. A freedom he attained through his acceptance of grace. It was through this personal freedom that Shuttlesworth sought to help others realize and accept their own freedom, so they could breathe freely, expand their horizons, soar with eagles, and swim in the depths of endless possibilities. Perhaps the apostle Paul had people like Fred Shuttlesworth in mind when he submitted his letter to the church at Corinth, "But by the grace of God I am what I am, and His grace toward me did not prove vain; but I labored even more than all of them, yet not I, but the grace of God with me" 1 Corinthians 15:10 (NASB).

God's awakening, invigorating grace changed the perspective of many throughout the difficult times of the Civil Rights Movement. And let it be known that step by step, grace energized the Reverend Fred Shuttlesworth in his persistent journey, and with singular courage, he fired the imagination and raised the hopes of an oppressed people. May the grace of God continue to guide you, my friend; you were, and will continue to be "our" warrior.

Notes

Chapter Two

16   Oxmoor had been: Lewis W. Jones, Indigenous Leader, p. 117.

17   Townsend, born in Port Tampa, FL: Susan H. Boyd, The Birmingham News, March 13, 1988, p. 96.

17   He joined The News: Ibid., p. 91.

17   He moved through: Ibid.

17   During the 1950s: Robert Norrell, The Birmingham News, March 13, 1988, p. 91.

17   The News support: Ibid, p. 96.

Chapter Three

21   Int. Fred Shuttlesworth, August 21, 1996.

Chapter Four

27   Int. Fred Shuttlesworth, August 21, 1996.

Chapter Five

36   Not only did the police: Telephone Int. Herman Poe, November 15, 1996.

40 In that arena: Jones, p. 133.

40 wait for another: Ibid.

45 Our aims: ACMHR Newsletter.

CHAPTER SIX

50 Int. Fred Shuttlesworth, October 14, 1996.

CHAPTER SEVEN

71 "Exceeded $50,000": ACMHR Newsletter, 1956-60.

73 Judge William Conway: Bud Gordon, The Birmingham News, March 13, 1988, p. 91.

73 James Mallory: Ibid.

73 Gober and Davis to testify: Ibid.

73 sent telegrams to the Police: Bud Gordon, The Birmingham News, March 13, 1988, p. 96.

73 Rilke to write: Viktor E. Frankl, Man's Search for Meaning, p. 78.

73 quote of Nietzsche: Ibid., p. 82.

74 Such was the case: Robert Norrell, The Birminham News, March 13, 1988, p. 96.

74 "ugly headlines": Ibid.

74   "extremists": Ibid.

74   Charles Brooks: Ibid.

74   The drawing showed: Ibid.

74   More than anyone else: Ibid.

74   the Times published: Ibid.

CHAPTER EIGHT

88   Miles College: flyer, "The Eleventh Commandments."

91   "4,000,000.00": Ibid.

92   watchman observed a white male: Telephone Int., Merit Stover, November 15, 1996.

93   Michael Langford: Telephone Int., November 10, 1996.

93   Connor yelled: Taylor Branch, Parting The Waters.

CHAPTER NINE

94   Lola tells: Telephone Int., January 4, 1996.

94   Shuttlesworth himself: Taylor Branch.

95   Carver High: Telephone Int., Merrit Stoves, November 15, 1996.

96   At one point: Taylor Branch, p. 757.

96   It's been a long time: Sam Cooke, RCA Records, 1964.

96   guns were capable: Taylor Branch, p. 758.

97   On a street: Ibid., p. 760.

97   helping whites maintain segregated negotiations: Ibid., p. 762.

98   King, after completing: Ibid.

100   Say that again: Ibid., p. 782.

101   What promises: Ibid., p. 783.

102   On July 25, 1998: Cassette Tape Recording, July 25, 1998, Southern Christian Leadership Conference, Jericho City of Praise Church, Landover, Maryland.

102   Fred's demands: Telephone Int., Lola Hendricks, January 4, 1996.

104   spoke in his old vigor: Ibid., p. 802.

104   being treated like cattle: Telephone Int., Herman Poe, November 15, 1996.

104   might result in federal legislation: Robert Norrell, The Birmingham News, March 13, 1988, p. 97.

104   The worst thing: Ellen Levine, Freedom's Children, p. 79.

107   I want this to be: Larry Still, Jet Magazine, October 13, 1963, p. 22

107   Recalling the horrible week: Ibid., p. 16.

CHAPTER TEN

110   Thirty-six years after 101 Southern Senators: Ibid.

110   Thirteen years after a task force: Frederick Kaimann,

             The Birmingham News, November 15, 1992, p. 2P.

110   Seven years after the land: Ibid.

110   two years after the city: Ibid.

111   Mayor Richard Arrington: The Birmingham News, November 15, 1992, p. 5P.

113   The voice of Mrs. Hendricks: Kathleen Henderson, The Birmingham News, August 11, 1993, p. 3W.

114   Odessa Woolfolk: Birmingham Business Journal, October 1992, p. 17.

CHAPTER ELEVEN

116   Herman Poe: Telephone Int. Herman Poe, November 15, 1996

117   We would often call: Int. Fred, Jr., December 22, 1996.

117   In 1965: Leslie Ansley, Cincinnati Enquirer, January 15, 1989, section E.

117   The conflict resulted: Ibid.

117   On Monday, June 2, 1969: Memorandum submitted by Lola Hendricks.

123 He had been struck: Cincinnati Enquirer, June 30, 1991, p. D2.

123 Shuttlesworth advertised: Telephone Int. Jim Flessa, Better Housing League, December 21, 1998.

123 On March 15: Ibid.

125 requested his support in protest: Allen Howard, Cincinnati Enquirer, August 28, 1995, p. A6.

125 Adarand vs. Pena: Ibid

125 Shuttlesworth argues: Ibid.

126 with singular courage: Fred Shuttlesworth statute, Civil Rights Institute.

MAJOR WORKS CITED IN NOTES

Branch, Taylor. *Parting The Waters: America in the King Years, 1954-63.* New York: Simon and Schuster, 1988.

Frankl, Viktor E. *Man's Search for Meaning: An Introduction to Logotheraphy.* Boston: Beacon Press, 1959.

Levine, Ellen. *Freedom's Children.* New York: G.P. Putnam's Sons, 1993.

New American Standard Bible. Moody Press, 1975.

New Revised Standard Version Bible. World Tyndale, 1989.

Nunnelley, William A. *Bull Connor.* Tuscaloosa, Alabama: The University of Alabama Press, 1991.

Printed in the USA
CPSIA information can be obtained
at www.ICGtesting.com
LVHW091517080824
787695LV00001B/154

9 781681 623214